Spending Time

With Joanie

Joanie Buchanan

ISBN: 1719190852
ISBN-13: 978-1719190855

Book formatting, cover design, book design, and editing by Cindy Hyde, cindyhyde.com.

All Scripture quotations are taken from the King James Version of the Holy Bible, King James Version, Cambridge, 1769, unless otherwise marked "WEB" which are taken from The World English Bible. A Modern English update of the American Standard Version of 1901.

Printed in the United States of America

First Printing, 2018

Printed by CreateSpace, An Amazon.com Company.

Available from Amazon.com, CreateSpace.com, and other retail outlets.

Inquiries should be addressed to:
875 CR 811
Nacogdoches, TX 75964
www.TheRemnantPublishing.com

www.joaniebuchanan.com

DEDICATION

I dedicate this devotional book to my sweet husband and family. My husband Denver, who has been faithful to love me and pray with me in all circumstances of life. My family has taught me many valuable life lessons over the years. In the years to come, I pray this book will be valuable to my four children and to my grandchildren and great grandchildren that I love with all my heart.

ACKNOWLEDGMENTS

I have so many friends over the years that have helped me keep going with my articles. If it had not been for several specific magazine editors like Connie with Heart Beat the Magazine, who invited me to write articles, Bro. Nick, who used many of my devotionals, as well as globalchristiancenter.com, who also put some of my devotionals in their magazine. Thanks for your encouragement! I would also like to acknowledge and thank Cindy Hyde for taking this project and making it a reality.

ABOUT THE AUTHOR

Joanie Buchanan is a radio and television host. She is an author who has been teaching and sharing the Word of God for more than 40 years. She loves bringing knowledge and understanding about the Scriptures. Her excitement and enthusiasm are contagious. Her teachings are impacting, inspirational and motivational. She attended Texas Independent Baptist Seminary and is a certified Life Coach through Light University.

She currently lives in Branson, MO with her loving husband Denver and their son Matt. Joanie spends most of her time studying the Scriptures and teaching. When she is not on the radio, on TV, or ministering she enjoys traveling, spending precious time with her family, and visiting with her many friends.

You can schedule Joanie through her website
Joaniebuchanan.com
Facebook.com/joaniebuchanan
Twitter.com/joaniebuchanan
joaniebuchanan@yahoo.com

INTRODUCTION

We are instructed to "Study to shew thyself approved unto God, a workman that needeth not to be ashamed, rightly dividing the word of truth." 2 Timothy 2:15. My prayer is as you read through the devotionals I compiled for you from 23 years of teachings, you will be encouraged, and blessed.

Your life's journey is ahead of you. Let's do some traveling together on this journey of Life as you read each weekly devotional.

Every day we fight battles, there are times in our lives when we have been hit by blow after blow that can leave us feeling crushed and shattered.

During these occasions, it is easy to lose all hope. God does not want us to live out our daily existence depressed or hopeless. In His Word, you can find comfort and assurance of His eternal blessings that gives us daily encouragement. Here is one of the many Bible verse for when you feel defeated. "For the LORD your God *is* he that goeth with you, to fight for you against your enemies, to save you." Deuteronomy 20:4. These devotionals will strengthen you for the journey.

Spending Time

With Joanie

"Oh God, that I would be
a woman clothed in purity.
Help me live my life with taste
that is continually seasoned by Your grace.
Let my life magnify Thy love
and with memories
recollective of me it was only
Jesus I could see.

~ Joanie Buchanan

1

THROUGH IT ALL, GOD IS FAITHFUL (OUR SON MATT)

Scripture: Romans 5:3-5

> And not only *so*, but we glory in tribulations also: knowing that tribulation worketh patience; And patience, experience; and experience, hope: And hope maketh not ashamed; because the love of God is shed abroad in our hearts by the Holy Ghost which is given unto us.

Reflection: The passages of scripture at the beginning of this article can be difficult to understand and can certainly appear to be very complex. Test and trials do come and often linger much longer than we want them to. However, God will use them for His Glory and our good. That may seem strange if you're in the middle of something so horrible you don't know how you are going to get through, let alone try to see the purpose for what is taking place.

I know for me, there are times when it has been hard to understand why this is happening. In a moments time we find ourselves having more questions than answers and the emotions are so overwhelming that it is difficult to see anything good coming from it. But God is faithful, and I know it is in Him we must trust.

When our son Matt was several months old, he was diagnosed with the genetic disorder of Downs Syndrome. The doctor who delivered Matt told us only that Matt was premature. He later admitted to us, "I was not sure." As a young woman of twenty-four, the shock and disbelief that my husband and I felt was indescribable. Yet, at the same time, God's grace was sufficient to help heal and overshadow the pain of this revelation. My husband and I had never been around handicapped children enough to know what we were facing.

A few months after Matt's birth, I took him to a Christian pediatrician who explained Matt's diagnosis in terms we could more easily comprehend and comforted us with scriptures. God used this sensitive Christian physician to help us start the journey neither one of us ever imagined we were destined to walk through. Thankfully, our Christian friends and family gave Godly comfort to us, and our church family was such a wonderful resource of spiritual help to us as well.

My husband and I had been raised in a doctrinal faith that did not emphasize healing or miracles as a part of our spiritual lives. Therefore, up until that time of crisis, we loved God, but never thought much about God's power to heal and deliverance was something we had never been taught. We soon began to learn that

God's miracles where still for today. As we prayed we started to observe the fact that Matt was able to do things at a young age that was never expected of him. We were told that his life expectancy was only about twelve years. He is now 50 and is not on any type of medication. Matt has never had a heart problem and he speaks amazingly well. He loves to pray and quote the Word of God from memory.

We have seen him bring people to their knees in prayer as he quotes the 23rd Psalm, Psalm 100, and 1 Corinthians 13.

We have three wonderful daughters and eight grandchildren. We are all amazed at his extraordinary gift of quoting scripture. When our family gets together at Christmas Matt quotes Luke the second chapter; at Thanksgiving, he has a passage ready to recite for that occasion, too!

One of the things I love most about Matt is his unconditional love. He loves his three sisters I think more than they even realize. He spends much time in prayer for them and all those for whom he has been asked to pray. His deep compassion, love, consideration and manners have been a testimony to all who know him.

How can you ever fully explain God and how He sees us through obstacles that we thought we could never endure? I must say that over the years, there have been some tough moments, but the joy of having a special son like Matt has made those times easier for we not only know about God, we know God!

The psalmist reminds us,

"For my thoughts *are* not your thoughts, neither *are* your ways my ways, saith the LORD.

For *as* the heavens are higher than the earth, so are my ways higher than your ways, and my thoughts than your thoughts." Isaiah 55:8-9

I perceive, that all problems, discouragements, heartaches and pain are, in truth, great opportunities in disguise. As we look beyond the struggles and lift our eyes on Jesus Christ and not the problems, we can walk in faith and experience all God has for us. For with God all things are possible.

2

HEAVENLY GLOW

Scripture: Philippians 4:4-7

> Rejoice in the Lord always: and again I say,
> Rejoice. Let your moderation be known unto all
> men. The Lord is at hand. Be careful for nothing;
> but in everything by prayer and supplication with
> thanksgiving let your requests be made known
> unto God. And the peace of God, which passeth
> all understanding, shall keep your hearts and
> minds through Christ Jesus.

Reflection: Christ attributes become part of us as we surrender to His will.

Paul did not pen these words alone, they were God inspired by the Holy Spirit. You can find many verses in the Old Testament with the word rejoice. The word Joy or Rejoice is mentioned sixteen times in these four chapters. The Hebrew word for rejoice, it is 'simhah', which has as its root meaning, "to shine, to be bright."

So, the biblical phrase "Rejoice in the Lord", could well be translated Brighten up in the Lord always; and again, I say brighten up! The Lord is telling us to put on a happy face, smile, and allow the Holy Spirit to lift up our countenance.

A radiant face, a heavenly glow; should mean that we are committed to God and we have come to the conclusion that it is in Him we can have victory. His word says that "in His presence is fullness of joy." I will surely receive His full joy, how about you?

A downcast spirit will show up even on our face. We just have to face it, our joy is not dependent on others: circumstances must not rule. It is God who puts joy on in our hearts that shows on our face. He reaches way down in our hearts and makes us feel better.

The best pill for a heavenly glow is to keep the Good News of the Gospel flowing inside of us. Take in the Gospel every day; it is the good news that will strengthen our bones and make them healthy and cause us to glow with His presence everywhere we go. A heavenly glow will convince others that we have been with Jesus.

But we all, with open face beholding as in a glass the glory of the Lord, are changed into the same image from glory to glory, even as by the Spirit of the Lord. 2 Corinthians 3:18

His face did shine as the sun, and his raiment was white as the light. Matthew 17:2b

3

A GOD ENCOUNTER
(TRY AGAIN!)

Scripture: Luke 5:4

> Now when he had left speaking, he said unto
> 'Simon, Launch out into the deep, and let down
> your nets for a draught.'

Reflection: We, by faith, must obey the voice of God.
This treasured lesson has also become characteristic of
the mission of God's people.

This chapter of Simon Peter's life can surely identify
with times in our life, it does not always seem to be
going like we think it should. We say, "What is the use,
I have tried so many times and it is just not working."

That picture seems to be evident at this particular
time in Simon's life, he was tired and saw no reason to
pursue fishing any more that day. His emotions where
down, I am sure his eyes where tired, his arms where
hurting, because of no catch of fish, his finances had

probably suffered, he just wanted to go home! Then the Master walks up to him and says, "Launch out into the deep and let down your nets for a catch." Oh, how he must have said to himself, "I really do not want to do this, I have been there and done that, just let me get out of here, rest and forget about this day."

Yet, like Simon, if the Master asks us to do something we must obey even when we don't feel like it. God has a purpose in mind that will work out for our good and His glory. If we will just remember that faith must act and not react to what God asks of us. Jesus wanted Simon and his partners to understand that He provides all that we could ever ask or think.

What makes us think we know more than our Creator? Simon reluctantly responded to what Jesus said and not only did he catch a huge amount of fish, he needed immediate help from others to land the catch.

The catching of fish was not a personal matter only for Peter, others were invited to assist in the catch. If Peter had not obeyed the Lord that day, he would have missed out on God's best and others would not have received the blessing. It took the miracle of the fish for Peter to see that God would provide even when things looked impossible.

Simon's response brings him into the very presence of God. Jesus had challenged Simon with his own inadequacies in the very area that defined who he was as a person, "his profession." Simon was humbled here in the one area of life where he thought he should be in control. There are times when we think it is easier to push away, and not come face to face with ourselves. In Peter's moment of humiliation, he is able to come face to face with himself and confess, "I am a sinful man." This marks a turning point in Simon's life.

Jesus said, "Don't be afraid," As Simon lay at Jesus' feet, reduced to the humbleness of a child, Jesus responded with the grace and love of a parent reassuring a child who has lost all confidence in themselves that they still have value and worth. The incident here was far more than a miracle of fish; it was nothing less than an encounter with God that forever changed who Simon and the other men would be.

4

CALLING ALL MOMS

Scripture: Proverbs 31:28

> Her children arise up, and call her blessed; her husband also, and he praiseth her.

Reflection: A Godly mom is highly favored of the Lord. She is not one who is selfish; she displays a life of unselfishness to her family because God has taught her to love as He loves.

To show God's love is one of the greatest disciplines a mom can ever learn, yet it will predestine her to a life of honor and respect from her children. A mom is a prayer warrior fighting in prayer for her children. Moms are not perfect. However, moms can display godly characteristics through the power of the Holy Spirit.

There is a lot I would like to say about moms, but the page of a devotional does not allow me to do so. My cry is for all of us as Mothers, to listen to God's heart and be there for our children. Let them see godly attributes lived out through all of us as Christian moms.

It has been said that if we were given a generation of Christian mothers, the face of our society would change in twelve months. Lincoln said about his mother, "No man is poor who has a godly mother."

The one we should truly honor is the Lord, because He is the one who puts the qualities of godliness into Motherhood. Without Christ, there would be no godly mothers. He reveals and imparts to a godly woman how to live out His Divine characteristics. The godly woman knows how to dress modestly and communicates that to her children as she is the shining example before them.

I would like to call upon the words of a man named Lemuel in Proverbs chapter 31. He was a King who had a godly mother. God chose to put this chapter in writing. It has forever been etched into the ageless record of God's book, so that the sands of time could never erase it. The King left us with the counsel of a godly mother.

Every verse in Proverbs 31 is valuable; however, allow me to pull out a few verses from Proverbs 31:26-31 (WEB);

> 26 She opens her mouth with wisdom.
>   Faithful instruction is on her tongue.
> 27 She looks well to the ways of her household,
>   and doesn't eat the bread of idleness.
> 28 Her children rise up and call her blessed.
>   Her husband also praises her:
> 29 "Many women do noble things,
>   but you excel them all."

30 Charm is deceitful, and beauty is vain;
   but a woman who fears Yahweh, she shall be
   praised.
31 Give her of the fruit of her hands!
   Let her works praise her in the gates!

God has blessed women with one of the highest honors on this planet and that is to have children. God's word tells us that children are a gift from God. We get to love and nurture them for a short while, and then we watch them grow up to have a life of their own. Yet, our role as a mom is never finished when they leave the nest; we get to keep on praying and believing God to take care of them.

There is nothing as special as a mom who stays in prayer over her children.

5

COUNT YOUR BLESSINGS,
ALL OF THEM

Scripture: Philippians 4:6

> Be careful for nothing; but in everything by prayer
> and supplication with thanksgiving let your
> request be made know unto God.

Reflection: God wants us to be people who exhibit a
heartfelt thankfulness toward Him daily. Being
thankful when it looks like there is nothing to be
thankful for is a heart that knows where to keep its
focus, on GOD!

My husband and I were part of Underground
Evangelism in the late 70s. We traveled to different
churches showing films and informing Christians what
the persecuted church in Russia had to undergo for
their faith in Christ.

Every story that was told really warmed our hearts.
One story in particular stood out to me, it was about

an older gentlemen who had only one page out of the Old Testament. In fact, it was a page from Leviticus. Years later he was finally given the whole Bible, he fell to his knees crying and thanking God he could now see what was on the next page.

A Russian man who finally gets a copy of the Holy Scriptures after years of state-imposed atheism is more thankful for God's Word than we are for all the Bibles, Christian books, magazines and translations that overflow our shelves.

Some time ago I was reading part of Viktor Frankl, life story out of, "Stories, Illustrations and Quotes." It relates the story of Mr. Frankl and how he learned to be thankful in a Nazi death-camp. He said that prisoners in the camp dreamed at night about a certain set of things more than anything else, they thought of a nice warm bath, food and all the things that they had taken for granted. Frankl said that the prisoners around him began to appreciate beauty as never before.

In one especially painful paragraph, he wrote: "If someone had seen our faces on the journey from Auschwitz to a Bavarian camp as we beheld the mountains of Salzburg with their summits glowing in the sunset, through the little barred windows of our prison carriage, he would have never believed that those were the faces of men who had given up all hope of life and liberty. Despite the factor---or maybe because of it---we were carried away by nature's beauty, which we had missed for so long."

6

IMMANUEL, GOD WITH US

Scripture: Matthew 1:23

> Behold, the virgin shall be with child, and shall give birth to a son. They shall call his name "Immanuel"; which is, being interpreted, "God with us."

Reflection: This promise was fulfilled as spoken by the prophet Isaiah; in Isaiah 9:6-7 (WEB)

> For to us a child is born. To us a son is given; and the government will be on his shoulders. His name will be called Wonderful, Counselor, Mighty God, Everlasting Father, Prince of Peace. [7] Of the increase of his government and of peace there shall be no end, on David's throne, and on his kingdom, to establish it, and to uphold it with justice and with righteousness from that time on, even forever. The zeal of Yahweh of Armies will

perform this. This promise was fulfilled as spoken by the prophet Isaiah.

The true meaning of the season we call Christmas is, "God is with us." That is a true statement that should be present in our hearts all year.

God kept His promise when He touched earth in the flesh of Christ to save us from our sins and provide for an entrance into His presence. Wow, what love and grace He has shown to us. "IMMANUEL, GOD IS WITH US!" That is the accurate meaning of Christmas.

In this world in which we live there is so much attention on material things, an effort which pulls us away from Jesus and His birth. The principal objective of our devotion should be on Christ Jesus. He came to redeem mankind from the slavery of sin. He lovingly demonstrated His magnificent grace and incredible love with His presence among us. It is the most awesome miracle of all times. "Immanuel, God with Us."

The Old and New Testament tells us of Jesus birth, about the baby in the manger who is the son of David, the Messiah. He is the eternal Son of God, conceived by the Spirit and born of the Virgin Mary, in whom all peoples on earth are blessed. I just wish everyone would understand and embrace Him.

"Immanuel" is a word of assurance among God's people; it gives us hope. Whatever the conditions become, we know that God is with us.

Paul makes that real clear, in Rom 8:38-39 (WEB)

For I am persuaded, that neither death, nor life, nor angels, nor principalities, nor things present, nor things to come, nor powers, [39] nor height, nor depth, nor any other created thing, will be able to separate us from the love of God, which is in Christ Jesus our Lord.

He is with us NOW! Therefore,

> Let us therefore come boldly unto the throne of grace, that we may obtain mercy, and find grace to help in time of need. Hebrew 4:16

That is the message of hope for the Christmas season, all year long and for all eternity; God is with us! Therefore, with calm assurance that He is here, enjoy the season; plan big and love with the thought in mind that time is short-lived and we must enjoy whatever God places before us. Go light your world! God is here! Now that should make us walk with our heads up high with great confidence. We are not alone. He loves us. The God of all the ages is HERE WITH US!

> The grace of the Lord Jesus be with all. Amen. Revelation 22:21

7

THE ALABASTER HEART

Scripture: Luke 7:49

> And they that sat at meat with him began to say within themselves, Who is this that forgiveth sins also?

Reflection: If we're going to release the fragrant oil of worship, we must die daily and live a lifestyle of worship in the presence of God. We should ask ourselves these questions; Is God pleased with my worship? Do I passionately worship God? How much do I truly love Jehovah God? Do I live a lifestyle of worship?

True hunger for God will release true worship; when we are passionate people filled with fresh first love who pursue the presence of the Lord, it is then we'll experience God's presence among us. I have to say, "God I desperately need you every minute of every day." The outflow of that kind of life brings

Joanie Buchanan

deliverance, healing, restoration, forgiveness and cleansing. Worship that does not cost me everything or worship that does not involve brokenness and sacrifice is not worship at all! We must give Him everything.

We become humbled under His mighty hand, broken inside, and our pride is defeated. The games that life tries to push us into become very small in comparison to living in the Kingdom of God. Love rules and there is no jealousy. We see each other as brothers and sisters in Christ. The only title we are proud to hold is, "a servant of the Jesus Christ."

Our hearts are just like the alabaster box containing precious treasure soaked in a beautiful perfume. Brokenness helps us die to ourselves and our hang-ups; we can forget about ourselves and worship God with great freedom. It was only after her alabaster box was broken that the oil could be poured out, releasing its fragrance. Even after she walked out of the house there was still the lingering aroma; something had happened, someone touched God! The breaking releases the fragrance of worship. I love that!

Simon didn't think that he needed to be forgiven for anything because He was a Pharisee; he was religious and very arrogant. His title was more important than humbling himself before God. This just proves that he did not have a revelation of his need for God's mercy and forgiveness. That's why he did not have the passion that is necessary to follow Jesus. Simon did not know his debt; but the woman did. Here we see who touched God's heart. Simon highly esteemed himself.

This spirit is so easy to discern. Jesus blessed a woman that others looked down upon and Jesus highly esteemed her. This shows us the true test of a Worshiper verses a Religious Person. We must not forget the pit that God brought us out of. Remembering has helped to keep me focused. I would not have made it this far if it had not been for the mercy and forgiveness of God.

When we think it is about us, then we have gotten away from abandoned worship. Abandoned worship ushers us into His presence and allows the glory cloud of God to fill the atmosphere with something much bigger than what we could ever try to orchestrate. Like Job, we fall to our knees in worship even in the most horrific of times.

8

LIFE IS DELICATE
HANDLE WITH CARE

Scripture: Psalm 139:13-17 (WEB)

13 For you formed my inmost being.
   You knit me together in my mother's womb.
14 I will give thanks to you,
   for I am fearfully and wonderfully made.
   Your works are wonderful.
   My soul knows that very well.
15 My frame wasn't hidden from you,
   when I was made in secret,
   woven together in the depths of the earth.
16 Your eyes saw my body.
   In your book they were all written,
   the days that were ordained for me,
   when as yet there were none of them.
17 How precious to me are your thoughts, God!
   How vast is their sum!

Reflection: God made all the delicate, inner parts of our body. He knit us together in our mother's womb. Praise God for His workmanship. His great love and miracle working power cannot ever be matched by human hands.

A few months ago, the phrase, "life is fragile handle with care," became real to me once again. My youngest daughter delivered a precious premature baby girl. As I looked at little Eden, God reminded me of how fragile life is. That little one is totally dependent upon her caregivers. It is very important that loving care is administered to these little ones correctly, for it will assist in their spiritual and physically growth for years to come.

God has answered our prayers and baby Eden is doing wonderfully. Those first few days were certainly very critical but we prayed and kept our eyes on God. We knew that the highest way to help nourish life is through prayer.

God's love will walk us through whatever this life will toss at us. We are fragile, He is not!

I saw God carry my daughter and son-in-law through some very difficult days. Eden was in the hospital for two weeks and yet mom and dad lovingly stayed close by her side. Every day they waited and trusted in God; I must say His grace has showed up in showers of blessings. The day we heard she would get to come home was a great day of rejoicing for all of us. God's love through Eden's parents assisted in the support, growth and health of her fragile little life.

God knows our frame more than anyone else, He wants us to recognize how delicate we are and how desperately we need Him. We are like children in His sight, fragile and in need of much care and spiritually nourishment from His Holy Spirit. The Spirit of God daily sustains us.

We must be totally dependent upon Him. He is a perfect loving Father who knows all the answers for life, who could ask for anything more?

Prayer: Father God, help us to be aware of Your love and caring heart for each of Your children. Your word is a perfect reminder as to how we are to love, care and nurture the children that You have loaned us for a time, to help us walk as overcomers in parenting our children. We thank You for entrusting the children to us, we submit to Your authority and desire to be the caregiver You have called us to be.

Thank You for Your Word that says;

Behold, children are a heritage of Yahweh. The fruit of the womb is his reward. Psalm 127:3 (WEB)

May Yahweh increase you more and more, you and your children. Psalm 115:14 (WEB)

In the fear of Yahweh is a secure fortress, and he will be a refuge for his children. Proverbs 14:26 (WEB)

9

OUR DAD PAID THE FINE

Scripture: Romans 6:22 (WEB)

> But now, being made free from sin, and having
> become servants of God, you have your fruit of
> sanctification, and the result of eternal life.

Reflection: Pray that God will show you the cross and
what it means for us today.

As a little girl growing up I recall singing a lot of
songs about the cross. One that we sang often was,
"The Old Rugged Cross" written by George Bennard.
He said during his early years as a minister, he prayed
for a full understanding of the cross and its plan in
Christianity. He spent hours in prayer, Bible study, and
meditation, and finally he could see the Christ of the
cross as if he were seeing John 3:16 leave the printed
page, take form and act out the meaning of
redemption.

While engaged in a series of services in the Pokagon

Church, Michigan, he perfected his most famous and successful song, The Old Rugged Cross.

The first verse goes like this; "On a hill far away stood an old rugged cross, The emblem of suffering and shame; And I love that old cross where the dearest and best For a world of lost sinners was slain.

Refrain: So, I'll cherish the old rugged cross, Till my trophies at last I lay down; I will cling to the old rugged cross, And exchange it some day for a crown.

In Josh McDowell's book, "More Than a Carpenter," he uses a simple illustration to show what God was doing for us at the cross of Christ. He wrote, "An incident that took place several years ago in California illuminates what Jesus did on the cross. A young woman was picked up for speeding. She was ticketed and taken before the judge the judge read off the citation and said, "Guilty or not guilty?" The woman replied, "Guilty." The judge brought down the gavel and fined her $100 or ten days. Then an amazing thing took place. The judge stood up, took off his robe, walked down around in front took out his billfold, and paid the fine."

What's the explanation of this? The judge was her father He loved his daughter yet he was a just judge. His daughter had broken the law, and he couldn't just say to her "Because I love you too much, I forgive you. You may leave." If he had done that, he wouldn't not have been a righteous judge. He loved his daughter so much he was willing to take off his judicial robe and come down in front and represent her as her father and pay the fine.

Prayer: God we thank you for deliverance from the bondage of a life of sin.

10

THE ALARM CLOCK

Scripture: 1 Thessalonians 5:6

> Therefore, let us not sleep, as do others; but let us watch and be sober.

Reflection: There is a spiritual slumber in the body of Christ, some refuse to wake-up and acknowledge what time it really is today. The alarm is sounding!

Some time ago, I went to visit my daughter and planned to stay overnight. We visited and had stayed up quite late that night; I became tired and was ready to retire. She graciously gave me the most comfortable bed in her home. After reading for a while, I was preparing to settle down for the night. It did not take long for me to drift off into a peaceful slumber.

Very early in the morning the alarm that was sitting on a bedside table where I was sleeping went off with a loud annoying sound. Quickly, I rolled over and started fumbling to shut the loud sound off. My plans had been to sleep in a while longer; I did not want to get up at 5:30 in the morning. As a matter of fact, I was very angry that that alarm had disturbed my sleep.

This incident later reminded me of the prophetic alarm that is sounding; while some prepare to sleep through the warnings sounds God is giving. People do not want to be bothered with the sound of God's alarm clock. They in frustration will shut off the alarming sound of God's immediate warnings. God's people must stay alert and not sleep.

The Word has warned us that we must wake up the fulfillment of our salvation for it is much nearer than we think.

Prayer: God, Oh God, we call out to you to let the people hear the alarm clock that is has sounded in your Word. And it is being fulfilled every day in our Word. In Jesus Name, Amen!!

11

TAKE A QUIET TIME BREAK

Scripture: Mark 6:31 and Matthew 11:28-30

And he said unto them, Come ye yourselves apart into a desert place, and rest a while: for there were many coming and going, and they had no leisure so much as to eat." Jesus said this because there were so many people coming and going that Jesus and his apostles didn't even have time to eat. Mark 6:31

Then Jesus said, "Come unto me, all ye that labour and are heavy laden, and I will give you rest. [29] Take my yoke upon you, and learn of me; for I am meek and lowly in heart: and ye shall find rest unto your souls. [30] For my yoke is easy, and my burden is light." Matthew 11:28-30

Reflection: If you are like me there are times when you need to come aside somewhere and rest awhile. Jesus even suggests to his disciples to find a quiet place.

We get so busy in a world that can demand so much of us. That is the case in Mark 6:31; they had been so busy with the needs of others they had forgotten to take care of themselves. Jesus told the disciples, "Find a quiet place and take a break."

In Matthew 11 we are invited to come to Him for there you will find rest. The way to search for peace of mind is to find rest in God, His Holy Spirit comes along side of us and that gives us the victory and power to overcome.

The word "easy" in Greek is "chrestos," which means, well fitting. Jesus makes our yoke fit well, the life Jesus gives is not heavy, it has been carved out just for us. One has been quoted as saying, 'My burden has become my song.' Whatever Jesus gives He gives in love. Whatever Jesus allows comes with a light weight. Our enemy takes pleasure in trying to mess up our mind and make us think it is too much, I cannot take it. However, not Father God; His Holy Spirit will always give us the power to deal with the challenges that are set before us.

Find rest in your soul today, that place where we allow our mind, emotion and will to invite His presence. We then can sing with the Psalmist, "He makes me lie down in green pastures; He leads me beside quiet waters. He restores my soul." I assure you that you can find your song of praise and rest in Him. He is waiting, speak out His name and feel the pressure lift. Why not join me in a song? Let us make these Psalms sing for us today.

Psalm 28:7 Yahweh is my strength and my shield. My heart has trusted in him, and I am helped.

Therefore my heart greatly rejoices. With my song I will thank him.

Psalm 32:7 You are my hiding place. You will preserve me from trouble. You will surround me with songs of deliverance. Selah.

12

CAST YOUR BREAD ON THE WATERS

Scripture: Ecclesiastes 11:1

> Cast your bread upon the waters, for thou shalt find it after many days.

Reflection: God's acts of kindness through you will bring rewards that continue into your future. The good deed you do today may benefit you or someone else at the least expected time.

Will you stop and ask God to show you who you are supposed to reach out and touch with His love today? There is nothing more rewarding than giving a helping hand to one in distress in the name of God. Good deeds come in various ways, just let God tell you. Don't stop and reason, just obey God. It will make your day, there will be no time for the "poor me syndrome."

Our expressions of God's love will be remembered by Him. What we do as an extension of God's hand is never forgotten by our Heavenly Father. It is very important to remember that we do it as unto the Lord that is what pleases the Father's heart.

Casting out good deeds means to release it and let it go, in time it will find its way back. Isn't God awesome!

The story is told about a poor boy who was selling goods from door to door to pay his way through school, one day he found that he had only one thin dime left, and he was hungry.

He decided he would ask for a meal at the next house. However, he lost his nerve when a lovely young woman opened the door.

Instead of a meal he asked for a drink of water. She thought he looked hungry so she brought him a large glass of milk. He drank it, and then asked, how much do I owe you?"

You don't owe me anything," she replied. "Mother has taught us never to accept pay for a kindness."

He said ... "Then I thank you from my heart."

As Howard Kelly left that house, he not only felt stronger physically, but his faith in God and man was strong also. He had been ready to give up and quit.

Many years' later that same young woman became critically ill. The local doctors were baffled. They finally sent her to the big city, where they called in specialists to study her rare disease.

Dr. Howard Kelly was called in for the consultation. When he heard the name of the town she came from, a strange light filled his eyes.

Immediately he rose and went down the hall of the hospital to her room.

Dressed in his doctor's gown he went in to see her. He recognized her at once.

He went back to the consultation room determined to do his best to save her life. From that day he gave special attention to her case.

After a long struggle, the battle was won.

Dr. Kelly requested the business office to pass the final bill to him for approval. He looked at it, and then wrote something on the edge and the bill was sent to her room. She feared to open it, for she was sure it would take the rest of her life to pay for it all. Finally, she looked, and something caught her attention on the side of the bill. She read these words ...

"Paid in full with one glass of milk."

(Signed) Dr. Howard Kelly.

Tears of joy flooded her eyes as her happy heart prayed: "Thank You, God that your love has spread abroad through human hearts and hands."

Prayer: Thank You Father God that today we as Your children are reminded that life should be lived like the Good Samaritan. Help us to find our hands doing what You tell us from our heart. We will not put our acts of Kindness on display, we hand it all to You in the name of the Lord our God. Speak to us and give us direction. Father who needs us today to be your hand extended today?

13

WHERE IS YOUR FOCUS

Scripture: Matthew 7:2 and Galatians 6:7-8

> For with what judgment ye judge, ye shall be judged: and with what measure ye mete, it shall be measured to you again.

We will reap what we sow.

> Be not deceived; God is not mocked: for whatsoever a man soweth, that shall he also reap. For he that soweth to his flesh shall of the flesh reap corruption; but he that soweth to the Spirit shall of the Spirit reap life everlasting. Galatians 6:7-8

Reflection: If you are swift and harsh in judging others, then you will receive the same from others. "Wouldn't it be amazing if every Christian actually took time to judge themselves before judging anyone else?

In Matthew 7:4-5, Jesus says,

> "Or how wilt thou say to thy brother, Let me pull out the mote out of thine eye; and, behold, a beam is in thine own eye? Thou hypocrite, first cast out the beam out of thine own eye; and then shalt thou see clearly to cast out the mote out of thy brother's eye." A good judge will not fail to judge himself.

As you know, we cannot pick and choose the verses we want to make a case when studying the Bible. I have to collect all the verses I can on a given subject and then see how it reads in the context of the passage.

Jesus tells us to examine ourselves first before we look at others. By focusing on ourselves, I firmly believe we can easily understand who we are and easily point out the weak area and eventually can encourage and motivate our self to refine our attitude. Our character and relationship with other people helps us to spread the love and kindness of our Lord Jesus Christ.

We can be too quick to find the mistakes of others and point out what they are doing wrong; however, does this make us feel better if we look at others instead of looking internally within ourselves? If we would just talk to God first and let Him show us our path of life, I think we would be much more concerned about what He wants us to do than always finding fault with others.

As God's Child, if we submit to Him, we would not have to live with a critical and judgmental spirit, which means that imbedded within are some internal problems that must be confronted and prayed about to deliver us from bondage. We all have to watch being judgmental for it will quench the Holy Spirit in our lives.

Prayer: Father God, let us see through Your eyes and not through our own flesh, then our perspective on life would be much more discerning. We ask for wisdom today.

14

VISIONARIES

Scripture: Joshua 1:3

> Every place that the sole of your foot shall tread upon, that have I given unto you, as I said unto Moses."

Reflection: Joshua and Caleb on the other side of the cross had more understanding of God's provisions and promises for them than some of us today.

God called faithful Joshua and told him in Joshua 1:3, Every place that the sole of your foot will tread upon I have given you. As I said to Moses."

> Only be strong and very courageous. Be careful to observe to do according to all the law, which Moses my servant commanded you. Don't turn from it to the right hand or to the left, that you may have good success wherever you go. [8] This book of the law shall not depart from your mouth, but you shall

meditate on it day and night, that you may observe to do according to all that is written in it; for then you shall make your way prosperous, and then you shall have good success. [9] Haven't I commanded you? Be strong and courageous. Don't be afraid. Don't be dismayed, for Yahweh your God is with you wherever you go."" Praise God that is a great promise for a winning attitude! Joshua 1:7-9 (WEB)

Joshua and Caleb on the other side of the cross had more understanding of God's provisions and promises for them than some of us today. God had said, "I will give you Canaan." Joshua and Caleb believed God and became visionaries rather than men with a hopeless attitude. They left a legacy that we are still reading about today. It will give confidence to your faith if you will stand on the promises of God by reading and believing His Word.

As you seek to live above and beyond the level of the majority, God will change you.

When the twelve spies investigated the land of Canaan, ten became very disappointed at what they saw with their eyes. They said, "There are giants in the land of Canaan." They completely dismissed that God had said, "I will give you the land." We know that they did encounter some battles along the journey. However, God did promise them the land and also promised to be with them. You can be sure that God always keeps His promise.

The Israelites saw only with one set of eyes, the natural. However, Joshua and Caleb saw beyond the natural into the spiritual promises of God. The two (Joshua and Caleb) said "we are well able." Two saw the size of their God and ten saw the size of men; two saw the solution, but ten saw the problem; two saw the appointment; however, ten saw it as a disappointment. Joshua and Caleb were willing to go against the majority. Years later God granted only these two men permissions to go into the promise land (Canaan). Believe me, God rewards His faithful servants.

There are some days that are disappointments; however, God turned them into appointments.

There is a lot said about getting started, but what about those who endure and finish the course?

Prayer: God we need help to win this race of life. Day by day we travel this journey and with calm assurance it is good to know that You God, are a Perfect and Holy God.

15

WAKE UP CHURCH!

Scripture: Revelation 3:16-22 (WEB)

So, because you are lukewarm, and neither hot nor cold, I will vomit you out of my mouth. [17] Because you say, 'I am rich, and have gotten riches, and have need of nothing;' and don't know that you are the wretched one, miserable, poor, blind, and naked; [18] I counsel you to buy from me gold refined by fire, that you may become rich; and white garments, that you may clothe yourself, and that the shame of your nakedness may not be revealed; and eye salve to anoint your eyes, that you may see. [19] As many as I love, I reprove and chasten. Be zealous therefore, and repent. [20] Behold, I stand at the door and knock. If anyone hears my voice and opens the door, then I will come in to him, and will dine with him, and he with me. [21] He who overcomes, I will give to him to sit down with me on my throne, as I also overcame, and sat down with my Father on his throne. [22] He who has an ear, let him hear what the Spirit says to the assemblies.'"

John was left forsaken on the island called Patmos, but God never left him. In John's time of abandonment on some of the worse piece of property; God showed him things to come. In this particular chapter, John was told to write what he saw and send it to the seven churches of Asia.

The seventh and last church was the Laodicean Church, which seems to represents the coldest and hardest of all the churches. They had left their first love. The first and greatest commandment is to, 'love the Lord thy God with all of our heart, mind and soul."

Being cold in this passage speaks of being formal or without spiritual life. Lukewarm represents straddling the fence or indifference, as having religion but not a relationship with Christ. Hot would represent that believer that has a passionate love for Christ and walks in the path God has ordained for them.

This Church had grown indifferent in their commitment to God. Satan had deceived them into thinking they were in need of nothing. The church was self-absorbed and self-satisfied, they thought that outward riches made them righteous. They were high on the social record; they had bank accounts, investments, you name it, they were at the top of the list. However, the Gospel was not being preached and truth had been abandoned. Inside Laodicea was the poor and the blind.

The Wakeup Call is here! It is unfortunate, but many in our churches are making the same mistake as the Laodicean Church. Materialism and greed is so rampant in our world today. Some church members have been lulled to sleep by a pill called materialism. Like today, this church had been blinded by Satan; Christ said they needed eye salve so that they might see. The Holy Spirit is the only one that can give clear vision. The enemy will distract us and make us think we are OK when we are not, we must wake up and stay alert!

This proves that you cannot measure God's kingdom by how much you have on this earth. Man will look on the outward appearance but God sees the heart. It is not bad to have material things, as long as you recognize that they came from God and therefore must use what He has given us wisely.

There is a way back for those who have left God out of worship. The Lord said to 'REPENT." But we must hurry! Judgment will fall for our disobedience to put God first.

Prayer: Father in the name of Jesus let us wake up to the times. Make us aware of You love and open our eyes to the price You payed for us to receive it. Help us to get off of the fence and turn back to our first love, the one true and living God.

16

WHAT WOULD YOU DO?

Scripture: 2 Kings 5:1-3

> Now Naaman, captain of the host of the king of Syria, was a great man with his master, and honourable, because by him the Lord had given deliverance unto Syria: he was also a mighty man in valour, but he was a leper. 2 And the Syrians had gone out by companies, and had brought away captive out of the land of Israel a little maid; and she waited on Naaman's wife. 3 And she said unto her mistress, Would God my lord were with the prophet that is in Samaria! for he would recover him of his leprosy.

Reflection: Naaman's wife went in hast to tell Naaman what the little girl had said. How could it be that a young servant girl from Israel could make a difference in a foreign land? God used her faith to bring about change in ways that no one else could.

Immediately, he started making preparations with his servants to go to the land of Israel.

Now, would that be enough evidence to prove he was acting in faith and would that help him get healed. Apparently not, God knows way deep down inside of us how many steps we must take to surrender and say, "Whatever you ask Lord, I will do it." in order to be healed. It did not start at the River Jordon. God first planted the plan in the heart of a little servant girl, captured from Israel.

After Naaman finally found Elisa I suppose he thought because of who he was that Elisa would be honored that he came to him to be healed, after all, Naaman was a very prominent man. Not so, Naaman had to learn that it was not about him, it was about the Lord receiving all the glory.

Too many of us want a miracle, yet we have preconceived ideas as to how it will happen. The Bible says that

> Naaman came with his horses and his chariots and stood at the doorway of the house of Elisha. Elisha sent a messenger to him, saying, "Go and wash in the Jordan seven times, and your flesh will be restored to you and you will be clean." But Naaman was furious and went away in a rage, "Behold, I thought, 'He will surely come out to me and stand and call on the name of the LORD his God, and wave his hand over the place and cure the leper.' (2 Kings 5:10-14)

He was angry and was going to go back home. However, this time God uses Naaman's servants to speak to him and they said, "My father, had the prophet told you to do some great thing, would you not have done it? How much more then, when he says to you, 'Wash, and be clean'?" So he went down and dipped himself seven times in the Jordan, according to the word of the man of God; and his flesh was restored like the flesh of a little child and he was clean."

We see God used Naaman's servants to convince him to dip seven times in the muddy Jordan. It started with a servant girl and ended up with his servants compelling him to obey the prophet in Israel. What would you have done? Or, should I say, what is your response today when God requests of you things that do not look or seem sensible. God often tells us to do the impractical to see if we are serious. He will tell us to follow a plan, one that does not make sense to us; yet, the outcome is for our good and God's ultimate Glory.

I can imagine that Naaman was taught more about himself that day than he ever knew before. God can and will teach us awesome lessons we just need to listen and be attentive to what He is telling us. It thrills me to see how God will use the most unlikely candidate to teach us life lessons. Be very careful who you call insignificant, too often we esteem the Saul's and dismiss the David's.

The Bible tells us that pride will go before a fall. God's Holy Spirit knows just how to get to the root of our sinful pride and show us how to be an overcomer.

17

ORPHANAGE OF SIN

Scripture: John 8:32

> And ye shall know the truth, and the truth shall make you free.

Reflection: The only way to seek fulfillment in this life is to allow God to break the chains of darkness and live in freedom from bondage in the Kingdom of God. We must not forget the pit that God brought us from and remember to Praise Him we are set free, if we belong to His family.

My heart weighs heavy over the sins of the world and how many people fail to submit to God's Spirit. Many years ago, while I was teaching a class in Dallas, the Lord opened my eyes as I envisioned masses of humanity lost in agony and bondage. It was then the Lord revealed the analogy of the Orphanage of Sin. The Lord showed me people as orphans without a home or family. They were seeking fulfillment in all the wrong places. Many of them were chained in cold and dark prison cells. However, as the cloud of deception lifted from the hearts of those who accepted the love of God's Son, their chains fell off and they were set free from their bondage.

My mind flashed back to the time God delivered me from the place I refer to as my Orphanage of Sin. I remembered the pain in my life as I searched aimlessly until I surrendered to the God of creation, who is now the Lover of my soul. At that time, I was unhappy and incapable of finding peace and direction in my life. God's Holy Spirit revealed to me that He had a wonderful plan for me. He promised, if I agreed to His plan that I would be transformed and live in a brand-new home, "The Mansion of Righteousness." Immediately, I accepted His wonderful plan of deliverance, at that very moment, my bondage was lifted and I was transformed.

I knew that my past life of sin was washed clean by the blood of Jesus Christ as a transformation took place in my heart. I ask God to forgive me of my sins and submitted to His plan. My life became brand new. He gave me purpose and I was ready to move on with my new life and my future.

He set me free from my Old Orphanage of Sin and gave me a brand-new home, "The Mansion of Righteousness." Right then, I just bowed on my knees and thanked God for Calvary.

Thanks to Calvary, I do not live in my Old Orphanage of Sin anymore. I am now set free by the power of God.

Jesus has openly displayed His love to the whole world by shedding His blood on that old rugged cross. His acts of love for mankind defeated the powers of darkness and the chains of bondage. The Word says,

> For God so loved the world that He gave His only begotten Son, and that whosoever believes in Him should not parish but have everlasting life. John 3:16

Praise God for the Love of God.

18

PRAYER, COMMUNION WITH THE FATHER

Scripture: James 5:16

The effective prayer of a righteous man can accomplish much.

Reflection: As a child of God, the most rewarding treasure is that we have been given the privilege of coming into His presence. Paul expressed his heart when he said in Philippians 3:8 (WEB)

"Yet indeed I also count all things loss for the excellence of the knowledge of Christ Jesus my Lord, for whom I have suffered the loss of all things, and count them as rubbish, that I may gain Christ."

Mary of Bethany set the example for us when she made the life changing decision to sit at the feet of her beloved Savior instead of first getting involved with earthly activities. Mary knew from that humble position she could receive all God had for her.

Do we want to know His heart, His will, to know who He is? In communion with our Father we discover that we are loved and accepted by Him. If we do not spend time with Him we will fail to recognize how special we are and how much He loves us. Love rules at God's throne. You cannot embrace God and not embrace His love. There is no prejudice there, no pride nor jealously. The only title there is God and His children that have committed their lives to serve.

Shall we travel the journey of prayer together enjoying what He says personally to each of our hearts? Let's arise from our bed of doubt and walk as whole men and women. It can happen through prayer. Well, Friends, come aside with me and let's rest awhile. Let's go into the throne room and kneel before our maker and king. He so wants our undivided attention. He is waiting!

Prayer Has Unlimited Resources

We have been invited to partake of the unlimited resources of God. He has said, "Call and I will answer." Prayer is not confined to the laws of space; prayer can be launched in a moment, and at the speed of thought reach its mark. The power of prayer and communication with the Father worries the devil. Prayer surrenders the battle to God, and it puts God and all His resources against the enemy. We can stand and declare, "There is no weapon formed against us that shall prosper." (Isaiah 54:7)

For example, Joshua prayed and the sun stood still; Elijah prayed and heaven was locked and it did not rain for three and one-half years; Daniel prayed and God revealed to him His plans for the future; the church prayed and Peter was escorted out of prison by an Angel; Paul and Silas prayed and God shook the earth and they walked out of a prison cell. We can give example after example as to all the available resources to us through prayer. It is unlimited because we have an unlimited God who keeps His Word.

Persistent Prayer

Persistent prayer will be transformed from discipline, to desire, to delight! We will experience divine preservation as we put on the whole armor of God and pray a hedge of protection about ourselves, our loved ones and for whomever God calls us to intercede at that time. Persistent prayer will not give up.

Jesus gave a good example of unrelenting prayer in Luke 18:1-8 when He explained the parable of the persistent widow. 'He said man should always pray and not faint. This widow in the city kept coming to an unjust judge to take revenge against those that were trying to harm her. For a while the unjust judge would not take any action; however, because of her persistence he gave in and granted her request. Jesus ends the parable by saying "Learn a lesson from this unjust judge. Even he rendered a just decision in the end. So, don't you think God will surely give justice to his chosen people who cry out to him day and night?

Will he keep putting them off? I tell you, he will grant justice to them quickly. But when the Son of Man returns, how many will he find on the earth who have faith?" (NLB) Will we stay persistent when there seems to be no answer in sight? Our faith must prevail when we are under pressure and want to give up. To grow weary and faint is to lose faith in God's promises. The question is, "Will we keep the faith when times are tough?"

Beware of Distractions

Spending time with God is a choice we have to make even when our flesh wants to take another direction. We have to fight the good fight of faith and choose to spend time alone with the Father. We must be aware of the tactics of the enemy. He will do anything to cause distractions. We have to remember when we give him our time we give him our attention and our strength.

Prayer an Open Door

In the book of Revelation John was abandoned to the Isle of Patmos. It was one of the worst pieces of real estate on all the earth. No one was there to say, "John, I know how you feel." But heaven was there with him. John saw an open door to another world. Have you ever felt abandoned? Just remember John. Man may close his heart to you but God never will. God showed John an open heaven. He saw praises going up around the throne room and that was enough to renounce anything the enemy might have used to discourage him. Praise is the language of Heaven, and there is where we find God, for He does inhabit the praises of His people. I sense such an overwhelming joy in my Spirit to praise God and to be right there with them in the throne room.

> "After these things I looked, and behold, a door standing open in heaven. And the first voice which I heard was like a trumpet speaking with me, saying, "Come up here, and I will show you things which must take place after this." Revelation 4:1-11 KJV

We must look for that open door where God reveals revelation knowledge to us. In that open door John heard the praises around the throne, "Holy, holy, holy, Lord God Almighty, Who was and is and is to come!" "Thou art worthy, Thou art worthy." I choose to bow with John and see the open door. I choose to stand around the throne praising My God.

We can measure our depth in Christ by the quality of time we spend with Him.

19

OPEN OUR EYES LORD

Scripture: Ephesians 1:17-19

> ...that the God of our Lord Jesus Christ, the Father of glory, may give to you a spirit of wisdom and revelation in the knowledge of him; [18] having the eyes of your hearts[a] enlightened, that you may know what is the hope of his calling, and what are the riches of the glory of his inheritance in the saints, [19] and what is the exceeding greatness of his power toward us who believe...

Reflection: Royalty has come to us, let us not be guilty of saying. "If only I had known who He was." Do not miss out on what God wants to say to you by not believing what God has already told you. He delivers on His Word. Let Him come alongside of you and prove it by opening your eyes to more of His eternal Glory.

In our Scripture Jesus has been crucified and has

now risen from the grave. It should have been no surprise to any of His followers. He had already told them that these events would take place. Earlier that day, an angel appeared to the women at the tomb and announced that Jesus had risen. With haste they ran to tell what they had seen and heard.

Later that same day two of Jesus' disciples were walking home to Emmaus. They had more questions than they had answers. The disciple's spirits were downcast because things had not turned out as they had anticipated. The seven mile walk to Emmaus gave the men plenty of time to reflect and discuss what had happened over the last few days. Suddenly, Jesus came along and entered into the conversation. T, but they did not recognize who He was. Jesus began to talk to them about the Old Testament prophets and things concerning Himself.

On arriving at their destination, they invited Jesus to come inside and break bread with them. As Jesus blessed and broke the bread in front of these two men their eyes were opened. It was an ordinary meal at the dinner table where Jesus made himself known. It is in the everyday occurrences of life that we must invite and partake of the heavenly manna. His name is called, "The Bread of Life." The daily fresh bread from heaven will certainly keep our spirits healthy and nourished.

As quickly as he appeared, He suddenly disappeared from their presence! They said to each other, "Didn't our hearts burn within us as He talked with us on the road and explained the Scriptures to us?" They were so excited, they walked seven miles back to Jerusalem to tell the others that they had seen Jesus. In a few hours they had come from hopelessness to a new level of faith, after spending time in His presence. If they had not invited Jesus into their home their eyes would not have been opened. When the eyes of our understanding become enlightened, faith rises to a new level. It is so simple, and yet we can make it very complicated.

The story is told that the Queen of England went out for a walk, when all of a sudden it began to rain. In the short distance she saw a cottage. She knocked on the door and asked the man to borrow an umbrella. Not knowing who she was, the man was reluctant to help her. He thought that maybe she wanted a hand out. The next day she sent one of her servants back to the cottage to return the umbrella. The man was shocked and embarrassed that he had been so rude to the Queen. He said to her servant, "If only I had known who she was." You see, royalty had knocked on his door and he had treated her with disrespect.

The Spirit of God comes alongside of us and changes a painful moment into a hopeful tomorrow, like He did for these disciples.

Joanie Buchanan

20

A NEW SEASON -
THE RACE OF FAITH

Scripture: Philippians 3:12-16 (WEB)

> Not that I have already obtained, or am already
> made perfect; but I press on, if it is so that I may
> take hold of that for which also I was taken hold
> of by Christ Jesus. Brothers, I don't regard myself
> as yet having taken hold, but one thing I do.
> Forgetting the things which are behind, and
> stretching forward to the things which are before,
> I press on toward the goal for the prize of the high
> calling of God in Christ Jesus. Let us therefore, as
> many as are perfect, think this way. If in anything
> you think otherwise, God will also reveal that to
> you. Nevertheless, to the extent that we have
> already attained, let us walk by the same rule. Let
> us be of the same mind.

Reflection: Let us seek God not only for ourselves but

our family, our churches, friends, leaders, nation, and many other things.

I am blessed and thankful for all the family that God has given me! Yet, God has asked me to remind each of us that we must spend time in prayer for them as we face a very exciting and challenging year.

My thoughts are on the coming days that we will be facing in this year. God has pressed on my heart once again to live out Galatians 5:16-22; It commands us to walk daily in the Spirit. Our life will become our Worship to God when daily we surrender to Him, everything will fit together like a puzzle when God is our focus.

> But I say, walk by the Spirit, and you won't fulfill the lust of the flesh. 17 For the flesh lusts against the Spirit, and the Spirit against the flesh; and these are contrary to one another, that you may not do the things that you desire. 18 But if you are led by the Spirit, you are not under the law. 19 Now the deeds of the flesh are obvious, which are: adultery, sexual immorality, uncleanness, lustfulness, 20 idolatry, sorcery, hatred, strife, jealousies, outbursts of anger, rivalries, divisions, heresies, 21 envy, murders, drunkenness, orgies, and things like these; of which I forewarn you, even as I also forewarned you, that those who practice such things will not inherit God's Kingdom.
>
> 22 But the fruit of the Spirit is love, joy, peace, patience, kindness, goodness, faith, 23 gentleness, and self-control. Against such things there is no law. 24 Those who belong to Christ have crucified the flesh with its passions and lusts. 25 If we live

by the Spirit, let's also walk by the Spirit. 26 Let's not become conceited, provoking one another, and envying one another.

Do any of these verses strike a chord within your heart? Wouldn't it be beyond wonderful to look ahead with a determined heart to truly be submitted to the Spirit of God on a continually basis. We like Paul would say, "I am crucified with Christ, And Christ lives in me."

The Lord says,

Remember ye not the former things, neither consider the things of old. 19 Behold, I will do a new thing; now it shall spring forth; shall ye not know it? I will even make a way in the wilderness, and rivers in the desert.." (Isaiah 43:18-19)

As tomorrow dawns, it will be another day, a new opportunity, and once again another season to show our love and faith in Jesus to a world that so desperately needs the Savior.

As we journey forward, knowing that God already lives in the future and promises to provide us refreshment as we make the journey that is before us. I hear my Lord calling to make the most of our time as long as it last.

How long is the journey ahead? Only God knows.

21

REAL PEACE

Scripture: Philippians 4:7

And the peace of God, which passeth all understanding, shall keep your hearts and minds through Christ Jesus.

Reflection: We must be able to recognize true peace from false peace.

There are some people that will be misled by the anti-Christ and his new platform of peace. I pray you will not be misled. Remember, peace is not in a platform presented by this world system. It only comes from the Savior, Jesus Christ.

The Puritan Thomas Watson put peace like this: God the Son is called the Prince of Peace. He came into the world heralded by angels announcing peace; "On earth peace..." He went out of the world with a legacy of peace, "Peace I leave with you, my peace I give unto you." Christ's earnest prayer was for peace.

He prayed that His people might be one. Christ not only prayed for peace but bled for peace: "Having made peace through the blood of His cross." He died not only to make peace between God and man, but between man and man. Christ suffered on the cross, that He might cement Christians together with His blood. As he prayed for peace, so He paid for peace.

Do you have peace today, or are you living in chaos and confusion? The Lord will safeguard the door of our heart against turmoil when we ask Him. If we admit to God that we need Him and we cannot exist without Him, He answers by becoming our Peace. He delights in the fact that we come to Him.

You cannot find peace in drinking, cigarettes, a bottle of pills, food, houses, jobs, different partners, etc. There are many places we look for fulfillment, peace, joy, and love. But there is only "One Way", and that is through the "Peace Maker," Jehovah Shalom.

The key is not in seeking answers to our problems, but in merely seeking and worshipping God who knows the answer. I say this often, "It is all about Him and what He wants for our lives." He sees tomorrow when we cannot. Our daily decisions tell where our point of dedication is found. Are we looking for God's peace, or are we looking for peace in all the wrong places?

In John 14:27 Jesus said, "Peace I leave with you, my peace I give unto you, I do not give as the world giveth..."

The world gives us disorder, chaos, busyness and anxiety. Jesus makes it so simple. He gives PEACE. We must first ask for it. He left His peace for us as a gift, but we must receive it with faith and trust Him.

22

RISE UP AND BUILD

Scripture: Nehemiah 1:1-11

The words of Nehemiah the son of Hachaliah. And it came to pass in the month Chisleu, in the twentieth year, as I was in Shushan the palace, 2 That Hanani, one of my brethren, came, he and certain men of Judah; and I asked them concerning the Jews that had escaped, which were left of the captivity, and concerning Jerusalem. 3 And they said unto me, The remnant that are left of the captivity there in the province are in great affliction and reproach: the wall of Jerusalem also is broken down, and the gates thereof are burned with fire. 4 And it came to pass, when I heard these words, that I sat down and wept, and mourned certain days, and fasted, and prayed before the God of heaven, 5 And said, I beseech thee, O Lord God of heaven, the great and terrible God, that keepeth covenant and mercy for them that love him and observe his commandments: 6 Let thine ear now be attentive, and thine eyes open, that thou mayest hear the prayer of thy servant, which I pray before thee now, day and night, for the children of Israel thy servants, and confess the sins of the children of Israel, which we have sinned against thee: both I and my father's house have sinned. 7 We have dealt very corruptly against thee, and have not kept the commandments, nor the statutes, nor the judgments, which thou commandedst thy servant Moses.

8 Remember, I beseech thee, the word that thou commandedst thy servant Moses, saying, If ye transgress, I will scatter you abroad among the nations: 9 But if ye turn unto me, and keep my commandments, and do them; though there were of you cast out unto the uttermost part of the heaven, yet will I gather them from thence, and will bring them unto the place that I have chosen to set my name there. 10 Now these are thy servants and thy people, whom thou hast redeemed by thy great power, and by thy strong hand. 11 O Lord, I beseech thee, let now thine ear be attentive to the prayer of thy servant, and to the prayer of thy servants, who desire to fear thy name: and prosper, I pray thee, thy servant this day, and grant him mercy in the sight of this man. For I was the king's cupbearer.

One has said that Nehemiah was called, not only to the workings of his hands, but the workings of his heart. His name means, "Yahweh consoles." It would do us all well to take a good look at Nehemiah's life. He was unselfish and reached beyond himself to help restore the broken lives of those who were crying out for help. God touched one man's heart and used him to restore broken people. Please, do not ever devalue the life of one person yielded to God.

Question: How does it make you feel when you hear about all the corruption, hopelessness and devastation that grips our world today? Do you sometimes wake up in the middle of the night and sense an urgency to pray?

I hope your answer is yes! Such was the case with Nehemiah.

Nehemiah lived in Susa which today is modern Iran; He was the king's cup bearer which made him a trusted servant with frequent access to the King.

Nehemiah heard distressing news about the plight of his people in Jerusalem. They were continually being harassed by the local enemies; the walls of their city lay in ruins and they had no protection against their adversities. Nehemiah was brought to his knees in prayer and wept night and day. He petitioned God for several months. Nehemiah was broken over all the despair that had fallen on God's chosen people because of their disobedience.

As he prayed God challenged him for the mission. Armed with royal authority from the king, He left the comfort of his family and position to answer the call and challenge of God. He was used to bring about restoration to his people. Let's ask ourselves the question, "when is the last time we wept, fasted and prayed over the enemy's attack against our loved ones?

If we allow the enemy ground then the walls of our defense will also be broken down. Like Nehemiah, we must become concerned, with a compassionate heart. God will then put a challenge before us and give us the power to be committed and to complete the task presented to us like Nehemiah did. He obeyed the will of the Lord. We can bring down those strongholds and repair the wall of protection.

Are you up for the challenge to pray and obey the Word of the Lord? Wonderful, then come on, let's rise up and repair the wall of defense and take back what Satan has stolen.

Just talking will not build. Rise up and build!

23

SUPPER TIME

Scripture: Luke 14:17

> And sent his servant at supper time to say to them that were bidden, Come; for all things are now ready.

Reflection: One day we are going to be called home by Father God. He will call His children and it will be a great homecoming indeed. It will not be a left-over meal or something from the local market. This will be the finest tastiest meal we have ever eaten.

Supper time, when I was a young girl growing up was what we call dinner today.

I can hear those words calling me as strong as they were when my mother said them. They did not want me out after dark so she would go to the back porch and call, "Joan, come home, time for supper." I knew when I heard that sound I had better start making plans to get home.

Supper time at our house did not always consist of a big meal. Dad and mom both worked so we had whatever they put together when they got home after working long hour days. The local Dairy Queen a block away prepared a lot of meals for us. Or, Lindy's grocery store, which was also very close to our home. Needless to say, I was coming home to something to eat.

Mealtime was not always fun, all four of us had our seat at the table and that is pretty much where we set every time it was mealtime. We rarely took our meals into the living room to watch TV.

The one thing my dad did not like was for my brother and me to giggle and act silly during supper. He was brought up and taught that meal time was a time to be quiet and eat. Yet, there were times Larry and I would look at each other and start giggling. Probably because we knew we were not supposed to laugh.

As I look back, I have come to appreciate those times which were not as bad as I perceived them to be.

Yet, the most thrilling of all is that Father God will be sitting at the table with us. This delightful meal being prepared will exceed any feast we could ever envision.

The invitations have already been sent! Only those who have received the Holy Spirit will be allowed to attend this banquet. He has asked you for your hand and all have received their invitation. However, one must RSVP. The prerequisite for this supper is to know and love Jesus Christ. Excuses are not acceptable. (Luke 14:16-24; Matthew 22:1-14; Matthew 25:1-13).

In the Old and New Testament there are over 2400

prophecies of Christ's coming.

Christ has certainly given out enough invitations to let His devoted followers know that He has planned a huge banquet just for them. I cannot wait, I do believe it will be any day now!

Jesus said this, put this down. Matthew 24:14

> And this gospel of the kingdom will be preached in all the world as a witness to all the nations, and then the end will come.

When that has been completed, He will return like He said He would. The invitation of the gospel is being proclaimed throughout the world. Yet, scripture tells us,

> For many are called, but few are chosen. Matthew 22:14

> But small is the gate and narrow is the road that leads to life, and only a few find it. Matthew 7:14

My word today is to make sure you are ready for the coming of the Lord. We must accept responsibility for our lives because Jesus is coming back, and ultimately, we will answer to Him!

24

TAKE A WATER BREAK

Scripture: John 4:4-7 (WEB)

> He needed to pass through Samaria. 5 So he came
> to a city of Samaria, called Sychar, near the parcel
> of ground that Jacob gave to his son, Joseph. 6
> Jacob's well was there. Jesus therefore, being tired
> from his journey, sat down by the well. It was
> about the sixth hour. 7 A woman of Samaria came
> to draw water. Jesus said to her, "Give me a
> drink."

Reflection: This passage of scripture is one that should
impact our lives. Jesus demonstrates what real love
and compassion looks like.

Here is a woman with an undesirable lifestyle plus
she is a Samaritan. Jesus never intended to come to
earth just to teach life lessons without showing by
example. That will always be one of the characteristics
of a teacher after God's heart.

Discrimination causes hate that can bring all kinds of division. It will keep people separated from the love of God, not to mention the pain it causes in one's life. Jesus has come to break religious and prejudicial barriers that can take root in us, just like it did when He walked on this earth. By simply speaking to the Samaritan woman Jesus was paving the way for all mankind to see by example that this is a wrongful act that has been continued by mankind for centuries.

Jesus was willing to go through Samaria even though there had been feuding between the Jews and Samaritans for over four hundred years.

Jesus stopped at Jacob's well which was more than half-a-mile from Sychar where this woman must have lived. She was marked as a moral outcast and possibly had been driven away from the village well by others making her feel unwanted; therefore, she had to come to Jacob's well to draw water.

At Jacob's well we see Jesus loving not only in theory but indeed.

As Jesus dialogs with this woman, He asks her for a drink. He explained to her that living water was not at Jacob's well, but it was divine and comes from God. Jesus cut through her selective false worship and traditions. When the Holy Spirit is presented God can move on a heart and break down all human barriers. As the Holy Spirit opened her eyes she wanted that living water that Jesus was talking about. Jesus then compelled her to face her immoral lifestyle, to put on the new we have to be willing to let go of the old ways.

He met the Samaritan woman at her point of need. He took a natural setting and used it to bring a sinner to God. Needless to say, she found truth because Jesus took the time to communicate the Gospel to someone who was marked as unimportant by others. Your situation may not be like the woman at the well, but it is time to let go of formality and unhealthy lifestyles and drink from the wells of salvation. Praise His Name!

"She dropped her water-pot and went back where she was not wanted and told the people, 'Come and see this man who told me all things that I have done." The first thing she wanted to do was tell others about what God had done for her. Let me tell you what He really did.

He gave her His love in exchange for all the old baggage she was carrying. She just needed someone to stop by and tell her. We must lay down our water pot which represents natural temporary relief and drink of that living water that will cause us to never thirst again spiritually. God was there for her and He is here for you and me. She was thrilled to share what God had done for her.

That is the way I felt when I had a personal encounter with Jesus, I wanted to run and tell about the fresh new living water that flooded my whole being, and I did just that, "COME SEE A MAN." It was a brand-new day for me, as it was for this Samaritan woman. We all come from different walks of life, but Jesus loves us just were we are and puts us where He wants us to be.

How many thirsty people do we fail to talk to because we do not notice them as we pass their way? Every day we have appointments with destiny. There is someone that God has appointed for you and me to pass by and allow the Holy Spirit to quench their thirst with His living water. We just have to be available to hear and obey God. Ask God to tell you where you need to stop and take a water break. Someone may be coming your way that is thirsty for living water today.

God's Holy Spirit is like fresh water that will flow into our innermost being and refresh us just like a glass of cool water on a hot summers day.

25

FORGIVENESS

Scripture: Mark 11:25-26 (WEB)

> Whenever you stand praying, forgive, if you have anything against anyone; so that your Father, who is in heaven, may also forgive you your transgressions. 26 But if you do not forgive, neither will your Father in heaven forgive your transgressions.

Reflection: If we want a sound mind, it is imperative that we give all of who we are to God.

"Doing an injury puts you below your enemy; revenging one, makes you even with him; forgiving it sets you above him." Anonymous

Let us always keep in mind that the first word from the cross was a word of forgiveness!

It is imperative that we do an inventory of ourselves every day to make sure we have not allowed unforgiveness to take root in our heart. Our deepest love for God must be reflected in the way we love others. I urge you to do a check list now. Ask God to reveal your heart. What is the intent of your motives? What are the reasons for what you do? Are they self-seeking, or do you honestly want God's glory to prevail?

God reminds us in 2 Corinthians 13:5,

> Examine your own selves, whether you are in the faith. Test your own selves. Or don't you know as to your own selves, that Jesus Christ is in you?— unless indeed you are disqualified.

Faith works by love. The Scriptures tell us that love will cover any offense, it will cover a multitude of sins. God's love will not allow us to have a heart bound with unforgiveness, which will ultimately bring about breakdown and diseases in our own bodies. If you are bound today, my prayer is that you let God set you free!

Forgiveness is the heart of God. To be obedient we must in faith release it all to God and then we can, "Let it go!" However, our mind tries to overrule our heart and we dismiss the Word of God that says; "Love your enemies." Seek to look beyond the person and understand who the accuser really is. The Holy Spirit is here right now and He is wherever you are. He continually gives us the power to release, forgive and leave it at the cross.

You can be assured that there are no demonic forces that are powerful enough to stop God's love flowing through us. If God is for us, who can defeat what He has deposited in us? I admonish you, "Let it go!" Let go of all offenses and be healed in the name of Jesus.

As God's children, how much better it would be if we would just "Let go and let God." Letting go of "our own self will" means we can then embrace the fruit of the Spirit, the first fruit being Love.

Whatever the offense, whatever the pain, you must forgive the one who hurt you. As you are on the road to a new day, remember, you must forgive yourself also. God forgives us if we will ask. Now, allow the agape (unconditional) love to come rushing through you. Speak these three words and let it come from the very deepest part of your heart, shout it if you must, "I LET IT GO!" Now by faith watch God move on your behalf!

Prayer: Lord I surrender my all to you. I know that you alone have the power to make me whole. I ask forgiveness, if there is someone that I have not released to you, I do it right now. I will walk away proclaiming, "I have let it go." I praise you, that I now am free.!

Scriptures on Forgiveness:

Psalm 25:18 "Look upon mine affliction and my pain; and forgive all my sins."

Psalm 86:5 "For thou, Lord, art good, and ready to forgive; and plenteous in mercy unto all them that call upon thee."

Matthew 6:12 "And forgive us our debts, as we forgive our debtors."

Matthew 18:21 "Then came Peter to him, and said, Lord, how oft shall my brother sin against me, and I forgive him? till seven times?"

Matthew 18:35 "So likewise shall my heavenly Father do also unto you, if ye from your hearts forgive not everyone his brother their trespasses."

Mark 11:25 "And when ye stand praying, forgive, if ye have ought against any: that your Father also which is in heaven may forgive you your trespasses."

Luke 6:35 "But love your enemies, do good, and lend, hoping for nothing in return; and your reward will be great, and you will be sons of the Most High. For He is kind to the unthankful and evil."

1 John 1:9 "If we confess our sins, he is faithful and just to forgive us our sins, and to cleanse us from all unrighteousness."

FAILURE TO FORGIVE DESTROYS ONE'S OWN LINK TO FORGIVENESS.

26

CORDS OF LOVE

Scripture: Hosea 11:4

> I drew them with cords of a man, with ties of love;
> and I was to them like those who lift up the yoke
> on their necks; and I bent down to him and I fed
> him.

Reflection: The prophet Hosea said that we are linked
to God with cords of love, cords that cannot be
broken.

I have never liked critters but we can learn from
them. I am reminded of a little story I read of a certain
spider. This kind of spider somewhat illustrates my
thought for today. There is a certain spider that builds
his nest in the branch of a small tree or bush. In this
fragile enclosed space, the baby spiders are hatched. If
the nest is disturbed in any way, the little spiders will
all rush out in fright. At once the mother goes to their
side. She is alerted to their potential danger in a most

unique manner. Each of the young ones has a thick silky strand attached to it, and all of these threads are joined to the body of the mother. When the babies are threatened by an enemy, they naturally scurry off, giving their lines a sharp tug. This is instantly felt by the adult spider. Within seconds she pulls them back to the nest where they are protected from harm.

Now isn't that just like our God. We are connected to Him that way. When we allow the enemy to frighten us, like the little baby spiders we scurry off.

Our wonderful loving God will pull us back if we are His child. When He says I love you we can know that He means it. It is an unconditional love that will keep us safe and connected to Him.

Thank God, we have a Father Who watches over us. Christ, like the spider's mother, will pull us back to a place of protection in Him.

Do you believe that? We are linked to God. There is nothing that can harm us, not even words of any kind. We have a Heavenly Father that links us to Him with cords of love. We are protected, no enemy can break though when we know our Father God is in charge!! Amen.

Give someone a hug today and tell them you love them and mean it. God's cords of love hold you tight.

27

AWAKEN MY BRIDE

Scripture: Song of Solomon 2:10-13 (WEB)

10 My beloved spoke, and said to me,
   "Rise up, my love, my beautiful one, and come
   away.
11 For, behold, the winter is past.
   The rain is over and gone.
12 The flowers appear on the earth.
   The time of the singing has come,
   and the voice of the turtledove is heard in our
   land.
13 The fig tree ripens her green figs.
   The vines are in blossom.
   They give out their fragrance.
   Arise, my love, my beautiful one,
   and come away."

Reflection: This time of the year always takes me back
to this verse in the Song of Solomon. He is calling the

Shulamite to awaken and enjoy the changing of the new season.

He has let her sleep long enough, now she must arise! Life away from His presence has been like winter. Notice, the flowers appear, as if they had been gone. The distinctive cooing call of the turtle-dove is one of the signs of coming spring.

This is a time of new beginnings; the cold hard days of winter are now disappearing.

A new and refreshing time has dawned; she must arise and come along. I hear the voice of Christ in these verses calling out to His Bride, "Rise up and go forward, Come Away with Me."

Springtime is an occasion for refreshing; it is a time to enjoy the beautiful surroundings, the fragrances, colors and all that God has given us to enjoy in spring. He clothes the landscape with enchanting bursts of colors, like an artist painting a portrait on canvas.

Just like God has determined seasons for us on this planet, so does He bring about seasons and changes in His Kingdom for us. It is our commitment to the Savior that allows us to meet these continuing challenges of everyday life. Our lives as believers in Christ are always a series of new beginnings. If we go to sleep spiritually we will miss out on what God is saying in every season of our life.

We must be ready for our roots to go deeper as growth comes with each new season. The Lord specializes in roots. We are often more interested in fruit, but God is also watching over the roots too. A gardener will tell you that if plants have a good root system they will flourish and grow. However, if the plant does not have absorption of water and good nutrients it is not likely to germinate and reach its full growth.

Whatever season we are in, whether it is fall, winter, summer, or spring, we can go through each change with assurance that God is with us. We can allow the fragrance of His tenderness to be a sweet smell. He wants us to grow up and be prepared as a "Bride adorned for her husband." Therefore, be ready for some changes in the days ahead. It is a new season.

God's alarm has been sounding and yet some of us appear to be in a deep sleep like the Shulamite. We must not allow the enemy of our soul to steal our time, when time is running out!

Awaken and come along! We must be ready!

28

THE WONDER OF HIS NATURE

As I have traveled all over the United States the Autumn Season never ceases to astound me. The season after summer and before winter is my favorite time of the year; I should venture to say it is my most cherished time of the year. It is always a must to pack my camera when traveling in October.

Every time nature sheds her summer coat with all its spectacular colors it is so breathtaking to me. There is nothing more beautiful than the Colorado Aspen trees when they turn into the most stunning variations of golden yellow. As the cool crisp air from the tall majestic mountains of Colorado brushed across my face, it was another reminder that winter was on its way. The voice of God in nature was saying, "Get ready for the change it will soon be here. The earth will transform into its winter coat until spring arrives."

Life is like that, we go through different seasons; But I have discovered that God sends us "Memos" that change is transpiring. We, however, fail to see or read the change, due to our lack of an awareness of His presence.

Why can't we be attentive enough to know that God is up to good in what He does and flow with whatever season He knows is best for us? We must remind ourselves that His purpose is to bring His beauty out in us so that all will look with awe and wonder just like I did in the Rockies and say, "God is to be praised." That is the ultimate goal in all things, "God is here, Praise Him! Praise the LORD, my soul. Praise the LORD."

My thoughts go to the magnificent chapter in Psalms 104. I shall end instead of beginning with some scriptures today. This is a beautiful Psalm. He beautifully creates with words all the wonders of our creator, God!

> Bless Yahweh, my soul.
>> Yahweh, my God, you are very great.
>> You are clothed with honor and majesty.
> He covers himself with light as with a garment.
>> He stretches out the heavens like a curtain.
> He lays the beams of his rooms in the waters.
>> He makes the clouds his chariot.
>> He walks on the wings of the wind.
> He makes his messengers[a] winds;
>> his servants flames of fire.
> He laid the foundations of the earth,
>> that it should not be moved forever.
> You covered it with the deep as with a cloak.
>> The waters stood above the mountains.
> At your rebuke they fled.
>> At the voice of your thunder they hurried away.
> The mountains rose,

the valleys sank down,
　　to the place which you had assigned to them.
You have set a boundary that they may not pass over;
　　that they don't turn again to cover the earth.
He sends springs into the valleys.
　　They run among the mountains.
They give drink to every animal of the field.
　　The wild donkeys quench their thirst.
The birds of the sky nest by them.
　　They sing among the branches.
He waters the mountains from his rooms.
　　The earth is filled with the fruit of your works.
He causes the grass to grow for the livestock,
　　and plants for man to cultivate,
　　that he may produce food out of the earth:
wine that makes glad the heart of man,
　　oil to make his face to shine,
　　and bread that strengthens man's heart.
Yahweh's trees are well watered,
　　the cedars of Lebanon, which he has planted;
where the birds make their nests.
　　The stork makes its home in the cypress trees.
The high mountains are for the wild goats.
　　The rocks are a refuge for the rock badgers.
He appointed the moon for seasons.
　　The sun knows when to set.
You make darkness, and it is night,
　　in which all the animals of the forest prowl.
The young lions roar after their prey,
　　and seek their food from God.
The sun rises, and they steal away,
　　and lay down in their dens.
Man goes out to his work,

Joanie Buchanan

to his labor until the evening.
Yahweh, how many are your works!
    In wisdom have you made them all.
    The earth is full of your riches.
There is the sea, great and wide,
    in which are innumerable living things,
    both small and large animals.
There the ships go,
    and leviathan, whom you formed to play there.
These all wait for you,
    that you may give them their food in due
season.
You give to them; they gather.
    You open your hand; they are satisfied with
good.
You hide your face: they are troubled;
    you take away their breath: they die, and return
to the dust.
You send out your Spirit and they are created.
    You renew the face of the ground.
Let Yahweh's glory endure forever.
    Let Yahweh rejoice in his works.
He looks at the earth, and it trembles.
    He touches the mountains, and they smoke.
I will sing to Yahweh as long as I live.
    I will sing praise to my God while I have any
being.
Let your meditation be sweet to him.
    I will rejoice in Yahweh.
Let sinners be consumed out of the earth.
    Let the wicked be no more.
    Bless Yahweh, my soul.
    Praise Yah! Psalms 104 (WEB).

29

A WINNING ATTITUDE

Scripture: Joshua 1:3, 7

> Every place that the sole of your foot will tread
> upon I have given you, As I said to Moses. 7 Only
> be thou strong and very courageous, that thou
> mayest observe to do according to all the law,
> which Moses my servant commanded thee: turn
> not from it to the right hand or to the left, that
> thou mayest prosper withersoever thou goest.

Reflection: Joshua and Caleb believed God and
became visionaries rather than men with a despairing
attitude. They left a legacy that we are still reading
about today.

It will give confidence to your faith if you will
stand on the promises of God by reading and believing
His Word. As you seek to live above and beyond the
level of the majority, God will turn your life around for
good.

When the twelve spies investigated the land of

Canaan, ten became very disappointed at what they saw with their eyes. They said, "There are giants in the land of Canaan." They completely dismissed that God said, "I will give you the land."

We know that they did encounter some battles along the journey. However, God did promise them the land and also promised to be with them. You can be sure that God always keeps His promise.

The Israelites saw only with one set of eyes, the natural. However, Joshua and Caleb saw beyond the natural into the spiritual promises of God. The two (Joshua and Caleb) said "we are well able." Two saw the size of their God and ten saw the size of men; two saw the answer, but ten saw the problem; two saw the appointment; however, ten saw it as a disappointment.

Joshua and Caleb were willing to go against the main stream. Years later God granted only these two men permission to go into the promise land (Canaan). Believe me, God rewards His faithful servants.

I know that some days appear to be disappointing; however, if you live devoted to God, days of disappointment can turn into God's appointments. Be aware that those around you need your healthy God-like attitude to help them find their purpose for life. Our approach to life can light a spark in someone's heart that just might reverse their negative attitude and inspire them to finish the course God has for them.

Visionary people like Joshua and Caleb see with two sets of eyes, the physical and also the spiritual. They know that a mind given to God can change their focus onto God and not their surroundings. That is why Paul could sing praises at midnight while in a cold prison cell.

He could also stand faithful before God when he

was beaten five times, shipwrecked, or stoned. He said in 2 Corinthians 4:8

> "We are afflicted in every way but not crushed: we are perplexed, but not in despair; persecuted, but not forsaken; struck down, but not destroyed...."

Surely you can agree with the Perfect and Holy God. He is El ROI --THE GOD WHO SEES ME. Now that makes you loved and very special. Take a moment to stop and rehearse all that God has done for you in the past and present. Then praise Him for what He is doing for you tomorrow as well. His Word says that you have an overcoming weapon, "The Blood of the Lamb." And His name is Jesus our Victorious Savior.

Now, if Satan comes knocking at your heart's door today, just send Jesus; He is fully equipped to handle the lies that the enemy is trying to place before you.

Are you leaving a legacy of one who can be labelled as an individual who had dreams, pursued them, and finished your God-given course with a winning attitude?

30

HARVEST TIME

Scripture: John 4:35

> Do you not say, 'There are yet four months, and
> then comes the harvest'? Behold, I say to you, lift
> up your eyes and look on the fields, that they are
> white for harvest.

Reflection: Tonight, I was reminded of a vision God
gave me several years ago. It was a picture of a golden
field full of beautiful wheat blowing in the wind. The
field was very large and as I looked further there where
plain clothed men and women harvesting the fields. It
was the most beautiful wheat field I had ever laid my
eyes upon. Everyone was in their place and seemed so
happy. They were working diligently to bring in the
harvest. I have never forgotten that scene. It has been
deep in my heart for years.

That is the way it is in God's Kingdom. He has
commissioned His followers to go and bring in the

harvest of souls from the four corners of the earth. Jesus is calling out to His children, who will go and work my fields today.

> Then he said to them, "The harvest is indeed plentiful, but the laborers are few. Pray therefore to the Lord of the harvest, that he may send out laborers into his harvest." Luke 10:2 (WEB)

Be aware, there is an enemy who will try everything he can to get us distracted from the will of God. He does not want us to be focused on God because then we would be, "world changers," in the Kingdom of God. Satan will do anything to cause us to waste time. Jesus never wasted time; to do the will of God is the only way to peace, happiness and power. It is only a matter of time before the Lord returns; we must be busy about our Father God's business. We must through the Holy Spirit recognize that it is "Harvest Time." It is time to move on God's time table and not ours.

> Sow to yourselves in righteousness, reap according to kindness. Break up your fallow ground; for it is time to seek Yahweh, until he comes and rains righteousness on you. Hosea 10:12 (WEB)

31

THE LIGHT HOUSE

Scripture: Matthew 14:22-23 (WEB)

> Immediately Jesus made the disciples get into the
> boat, and to go ahead of him to the other side,
> while he sent the multitudes away. After he had
> sent the multitudes away, he went up into the
> mountain by himself to pray. When evening had
> come, he was there alone.

Reflection: Jesus didn't tell the disciples all they would
encounter before they reached their destination. If
Jesus said they were to "go over to the other side," He
already knew they would make it to shore
safely. However, a storm arose into their voyage and
fear began to paralyze their faith.

In the passage we read that a storm suddenly came
up and their boats were battered by the waves. At that
moment their minds no longer recalled what Jesus had
said to them before getting into the boat, nor did they

remember the powerful miracle of Jesus feeding the five thousand that they had just encountered that same day.

When their boat became battered by the waves and wind, they cried out with fear. However, Jesus came to them mastering the sea, for He was walking on the water.

> But immediately Jesus spoke to them, saying "Cheer up! It is I! Don't be afraid." 28 Peter answered him and said, "Lord, if it is you, command me to come to you on the waters." 29 He said, "Come!" Matthew 14:27 (WEB)

Peter made a step of faith and got out of the boat. That is more than some of us will do. "But seeing the wind" he looked down when He should have kept looking up keeping his eyes on Jesus.

That is a Word for us today. Do not look around, look up, gaze at Who is in front of you; His name is Jesus, the Sea Walker.

Haven't we all been there? Or, maybe I should say how often have we been there? Don't you feel at times you are tossed into the sea of life not knowing how you are going to make it? You are having financial problems; you have lost a loved one, or they have become very ill, you receive bad news at an unexpected time, your marriage is slipping away; you have lost your job, and family issues cannot seem to be resolved

Keep in mind today, we serve a God who cannot fail and if we are trusting in Him, we can always be sure He will take us to the other side. God allows us to pass through (not always snatching us out) so that through the process we will learn to trust in

Him. Then once again He reminds us, it is God who must charter our course on this sea of life.

The words of our Lord echo once again, "You of little faith why did you doubt." His light will guide us by dispelling the darkness as we travel to our destination. HE is the Light House

There can definitely be peace and direction in the middle of the storm when God is there with us. Remember, what God says HE will bring it to pass! "Peace Be Still" as you ride out your storm.

32

PRODIGAL, COME BACK HOME!

Scripture: Luke 15:17-19 (WEB)

> But when he came to himself he said, 'How many hired servants of my father's have bread enough to spare, and I'm dying with hunger! 18 I will get up and go to my father, and will tell him, "Father, I have sinned against heaven, and in your sight. 19 I am no more worthy to be called your son. Make me as one of your hired servants."'

Reflection: This parable tells the story of a loving father.

What speaks loudest in this story is that the love of the father is much more than the sins of his son. A loving God is a forgiving Father. If you are in the will of God, let me ask you to remember to pray for those who are not. If you have ever left God, you know what it is like. I know I have.

Once Abraham Lincoln was asked how he would

treat the southerners after they were defeated and returned to the Union of the United States. Lincoln said, 'I will treat them as if they had never been away.' That is how the love of God treats us.

I think most of us have been like the prodigal or his older brother at one time or another. We could say this parable is about three people. The first is the prodigal, as the young rebellious and restless son who wanted to be on his own. Then we have the son who stayed, yet he was just as guilty of sin because he was religious and self-righteous. Finally, we cannot leave the Father out; He is the key to this story. The Love of God and His amazing grace is very real in these verses.

Jesus deeply portrays the love of God for his children in this parable of the prodigal. He reminds us that we can repent and come back to the loving Father who is waiting with open arms. We are welcomed home even when we turn our back on Him and fill our lives with substitutes or consider His ways outdated and society's ways more appealing.

His robe, ring, shoes, and a prepared feast are ready for the sinner who comes home. This homecoming causes much joy in heaven. If heaven rejoices, then surely the body of Christ can rejoice over the sinner coming home.

Please, do not let the enemy make you think you are a failure and that all your dreams are forever gone. Please, Wake Up! It is not over, the "BEST IS YET TO COME." God has allowed this to get you out of where you were, so He can take you where you are supposed to be.

God loves you!

The love of God is a common thread all through the Word of God. To miss it only says one has not read or studied His Word. Nor have they allowed God's Holy Spirit to communicate the Father's love. His love for mankind cried out all the way to the cross. Today, God's Spirit communicates and reveals to us how much He loves us.

This has been my message for over 30 years, God loves us, and when we mess up, He is there waiting for us to come back home. There is nothing else for God to do. He died, was buried and was raised the third day just like He said He would do. God's Word has given us love letters; do we read them in His Word? I have and am petitioning the Father for the prodigals. Please, prodigal, come back home!

Prayer: Allow the Holy Spirit to draw you to the loving Father right now. There is no pit too deep that God cannot bring you out of. May the love of God overpower you to day and open your eyes so you can see how much He really loves you. In Jesus Name. Amen.

33

A LOVING DAD'S FAITH

Scripture: John 4:46-47

> So Jesus came again into Cana of Galilee, where
> he made the water wine. And there was a certain
> nobleman, whose son was sick at Capernaum. 47
> When he heard that Jesus was come out of Judaea
> into Galilee, he went unto him, and besought him
> that he would come down, and heal his son: for
> he was at the point of death.

Reflections: How imperative it is to have a dad who
knows where to find the answers for his family.

In our scripture we find this man had the faith to
believe what God spoke to Him even before the results
were seen. This story touches my heart. Here is a loving
and passionate dad interceding for his dying son. This
dad kept persisting and believing when circumstances
seemed hopeless. The Bible calls him a Nobleman, a
royal officer of Herod's court. His position was one of

high priority.

Jesus was known as just a carpenter from Nazareth. Yet, this dad traveled about twenty miles to ask a big favor of a village carpenter. He inquired as to where Jesus could be found. The Nobleman found Jesus and begged Him to come and heal his dying son. Dads, like this Nobleman, who understand that Jesus is the answer for all the needs of their family, will hear from God.

Jesus made a statement in front of the Nobleman that might have caused some of us to turn around in despair and go home. He said, "Unless you people see signs and wonders, you simply will not believe." This royal official knew Jesus could help him and he continued to pursue for his son, "Sir, come down before my child dies." This dad would not be stopped or discouraged, he came for a miracle and he was expecting to receive one. Wow, I love this man's persistent faith!

This dad loved his son enough to not allow custom, or position to stop him from bringing his petition to Jesus. This is a true example of intercession. It is not the making of a petition but the taking of a position.

Jesus spoke to the man and said, "Go back home. Your son will live!" And the man's belief in what Jesus said caused him to turn around and go back home, for in his heart he knew his son would not die. Persistent faith in God will change our circumstances even before we see the results. After Jesus had spoken a word to the dad, "Your son will live" this dad still had not seen the miracle of his sons healing. He had twenty miles of nothing but Jesus' words to comfort Him. Yet, he believed that if Jesus said it, then it was not a matter of, "I hope it is true, but it must be true." Oh friends, to have that kind of faith working in our homes would bring a revival to this nation.

While the Nobleman was on his way back home, his servant met him with the news that his son was alive and well. He asked him when the boy had begun to get better and he replied, "Yesterday afternoon at one o'clock his fever suddenly disappeared!" Then the dad realized that was the very time Jesus had told him, "Your son will live." And he and his entire household believed in Jesus." Here is the greatest miracle of this story, the loving dads faith brought his whole household to Christ!

Prayer: God I pray that all dads will see how much they need to have the kind of faith this dad had. Break their hearts over their children that are dying from a lack of spiritual guidance. May they see like this dad, that persistence and humbleness will help bring about healing in the home? Let faith prevail and households be renewed in the love of God because of faithful men who know how to seek after God.

34

MINISTERING ENCOURAGEMENT

Scripture: Hebrews 3:13 (WEB)

> But exhort one another day by day, so long as it is called "today"; lest any one of you be hardened by the deceitfulness of sin.

Reflection: This verse indicates that we all need exhortation or encouragement daily. I know who I need to be around when I need Godly encouragement. We can remember the hurt of criticism after it is given. Therefore, we are encouraged to exhort one another daily.

Barnabus, who is called the Son of Encouragement in The Acts of the Apostles, saw how necessary it was to have that ministry; they called him Barnabas, or "Son of Consolation", which means "encouragement." A Barnabas is a very valuable gift to the church.

Before any kind of ministry, there has to be a relationship with Jesus Christ. We must be fully surrendered to His Lordship; this is the foundation for an effective and anointed ministry for service. A child of God whose heart is full of love and compassion will encourage others. It is God's love flowing from their heart to others. It is such a blessing to see and recognize how one's confidence is affirmed when words of kindness are imparted to them.

As we encourage others it will let them know that God is for them and not against them. They can be assured that God's promises never fail. God has deemed them special and has a plan for them to succeed. Philippians 2:3 tells us,

> ...doing nothing through rivalry or through conceit, but in humility, each counting others better than himself;

Remember we must encourage ourselves too. While David was in a time of heaviness and distress the Word says that, David encouraged himself in the Lord his God. I Samuel 30:6 (WEB)

> David was greatly distressed; for the people spoke of stoning him, because the souls of all the people were grieved, every man for his sons and for his daughters; but David strengthened himself in Yahweh his God.

I just love that verse. We must not forget Proverbs 18:21 (WEB).

> "Death and life are in the power of the tongue: and they that love it shall eat the fruit thereof."

Could it be that is a part of what you do. Are you conscious of the negative or positive effects that you have on others by what you say? God, I pray that you will sanctify our hearts and tongues!

Ministering encouragement to others is to exhort, affirm, give confidence, encourage, establish, confirm others, and esteem them above yourself.

Joanie Buchanan

35

JOY COMES IN THE MORNING

Scripture: Psalm 30:5 (WEB)

> For his anger is but for a moment. His favor is for a lifetime. Weeping may stay for the night, but joy comes in the morning.

This has been a very difficult day for me. I could not sleep Friday night and did not go to bed until 4:30 AM. We had to get up around seven. I just knew that after my appointments today that I could rush home and nap.

Well, I was mistaken. I is now 3:03 AM on Saturday morning and I am still awake. I can stay up but His is way beyond my limits. God has a reason and one is that I have called your name out this morning to God. And of course, prayed and sought God for myself as well.

Spiritually speaking, the night for some of you has been awfully long. You have wondered if God had just forgotten you (or chose not to remember! So, you wait hoping that tomorrow will be your morning of change!)

I know God is faithfully working behind the scenes as some of you lay broken before Him. From brokenness comes blessing. That may not sound too good to hear right now but it will make sense later.

Psalm 126:5-6 is a promise we can hang our hats on today:

> They that sow in tears shall reap in joy. 6 He that goeth forth and weepeth, bearing precious seed, shall doubtless come again with rejoicing, bringing his sheaves with him.

This verse reminds us not to ignore the restoration but also not to forget the weeping and crying that may accompany it. It even suggests that we serve while we weep, but not in place of the weeping. It will do all of us good to see the vulnerability and the honest authenticity that accompanies the tears that are not only allowed but encouraged.

People have seen enough plastic smiles to last them a lifetime. Emotional brokenness must be real, not fake. Christians need to be real so that our authenticity shines God's glory to a hurting world. No one needs to see a person trying to be perfect, but we all need to see the Power of God. When is the last time you were in the middle of a real encounter with God's Spirit?

In the story of the woman at the well, Jesus actually allowed the Samaritan woman to look back at her past, (John 4:18). The fact is, you have had five husbands, and the man you now have is not your husband He told her. A painful realization before bringing the healing that would allow "many to believe because of her testimony." I imagine there were some tears when she realized to whom she was communicating with and the fact that He already knew all about her.

Mourning and grieving are not events, they are a process. Processes take time. Prayer is a wonderful way for us to encourage the process. Don't be afraid of your own tears today or those of others.

I believe if the world cried a little bit more it would actually be filled with more laughter. Eccl. 3:4 says, "there is a time to weep and a time to laugh." Maybe we could laugh more if we took the time to cry more?

It's true: laughter is good medicine but so are the tears. Tears must be important to God. Psalm 56:8 (WEB),

> You number my wanderings. You put my tears into your bottle. Aren't they in your book?

> He will wipe away from them every tear from their eyes. Revelation 21:4 (WEB)

If He thinks it is important to wipe the tears, shouldn't we? Just remember: God can't wipe what we don't cry. Joy does in fact come after the crying and serving and weeping! Blessing comes from brokenness. Laughter follows tears. Restoration follows forgiveness. Joy comes from mourning.

HOLD ON CHILD, JOY DOES COME IN THE MORNING!! DO NOT EVER MAKE LIGHT OF YOUR MORNING COMING.

36

MARRIAGE SUPPER OF THE LAMB

Scripture: Revelation 19:9

> And he saith unto me, Write, Blessed are they
> which are called unto the marriage supper of the
> Lamb. And he saith unto me, These are the true
> sayings of God.

Reflection: My word for you today is to make sure you
are ready for the coming of the Lord. We must accept
responsibility for our lives because Jesus is coming
back, and ultimately, we will answer to Him! Please, do
not miss out on the greatest event in your life!

Wedding bells are ringing! The aroma of
preparations is in the air! Brides are scurrying around
making arrangements for their beautiful springtime
and summer weddings. Invitations are being sealed and
postmarked with love and excitement. Brides are
scanning through dress patterns and shopping in a
frenzy to find just the perfect wedding dress. Oh, how

I love the fanfare of weddings with all the beautiful floral decorations, table settings and, let's not leave out, the banquet table filled with all kinds of goodies.

There is another banquet that is in preparation at this very moment. This delightful banquet being prepared will surpass any feast we could ever imagine. The invitations have already been sent! Only those who believe Jesus Christ is the Son of God and accepted Him as their Savior will be allowed to attend this banquet. He has asked you for your hand and all have received their invitation. The prerequisite for this banquet is to know and love Jesus Christ. Excuses for not believing and not receiving the gift of eternal life are not acceptable. (Luke 14:16-24; Matthew 22:1-14; Matthew 25:1-13).

In the Old and New Testament there are over 2,400 prophecies of Christ's coming. Christ has certainly given out enough invitations to let His devoted followers know that He has planned a huge banquet just for them. I cannot wait! I do believe it will be any day now!

The invitation of the gospel is being proclaimed throughout the world. Yet, scripture tells us, "for many are invited, but few will come."

> How [a] narrow is the gate, and restricted is the way that leads to life! Few are those who find it. Matthew 7:14

I heard a story years ago about a very wealthy man from the east. He would go west every year to buy cattle, but this particular year he sent his son to take his place. On the son's arrival, they prepared a huge feast on the ranch so he could meet everyone and they could meet him.

In the crowd was a little servant girl who worked very hard on the ranch. However, there was something different about her that drew this wealthy young man to her. During his stay, he fell in love with this little servant girl. All the other girls made fun of her. They would say, "Why would he want someone like you?" Nevertheless, she and this wealthy young man fell in love.

As the young man was preparing to go back east, he said to this little servant girl, "I love you, and I will go back home and make arrangements to come back for you. Therefore, look for me, because I will be back."

Her love for him was so sincere. She worked very hard to earn the money for her wedding dress. All the while, the other young ladies laughed and made fun of her. They said, "He is not coming back for you." She paid no attention to their cruel words. She just kept preparing for her loved one's return. She had her beautiful wedding dress ready for the great event. Every day she would look down the long road to see if he was coming. Every day she lived for his return. Her wedding dress was laid out and ready for the special day.

One day, as she was looking, in the far distance she could see the young man coming down the road. He promised he would come back, she prepared herself and he did return like he said he would.

Have your wedding garment on and be ready to go. Jesus is coming back, like He said He would!

> Blessed are those servants, whom the lord will find watching when he comes. Most certainly I tell you, that he will dress himself, and make them recline,

and will come and serve them. Luke 12:37 (WEB) I heard something like the voice of a great multitude, and like the voice of many waters, and like the voice of mighty thunders, saying, "Hallelujah! For the Lord our God, the Almighty, reigns! 7 Let us rejoice and be exceedingly glad, and let us give the glory to him. For the marriage of the Lamb has come, and his wife has made herself ready." 8 It was given to her that she would array herself in bright, pure, fine linen: for the fine linen is the righteous acts of the saints. Revelation 19:6-9 (WEB)

Therefore be ready also, for the Son of Man is coming in an hour that you don't expect him. Luke 12:40 (WEB)

Turn your life over to Jesus Christ today, He loves you.

Prayer: Father God, in the name of Jesus I pray that you will cause ears to be opened and hearts to receive your son Jesus Christ as their Lord and Savior, right now. Let there be conviction of sin, need to repent, and the ability, by faith, to receive you. Allow the Holy Spirit to show them their need for you right now. Lord, fill them to overflowing with your Holy Spirit. Let the Power of God surround them and be in them right now, in Jesus Name!

37

MAKING MEMORIES

Scripture: James 4:14

"Whereas ye know not what shall be on the morrow. For what is your life? It is even a vapour, that appeareth for a little time, and then vanisheth away."

As I grow older I am more and more aware of life and how it must be seized. Tomorrow is only today as it passes by so swiftly. I hardly can take in 24 hours and then I find myself in another day. Where did it go? Times marches on, that is for sure.

There are times I like to reach back and pull up some of my yesterdays. It often is jolted by something around me that will put me back in time for a few minutes. I do love reminiscing at times. I cannot help but Praise God for walking with me through my past, present, and future.

Nostalgia is that yearning to step back into the time

tunnel and stroll down memory lane, trying to recover the unrecoverable. I guess that is why I enjoy listening to the older songs sometime. Here is where Nostalgia sometimes starts:

A quiet visit to the place where you were raised.

The smell of Christmas, the tree and all the trimmings.

Thinking how you met the love of your life.

Dating and getting to know each other.

Family and Friends talking about how it use to be.

Music and melodies of your past.

Singing the Song of your Alma Mater.

A barefoot walk along a sandy beach.

Looking over childhood photos will sure put you back in time.

A newborn baby.

An old letter, bruised with age signed by the one who loves you.

Climbing mountains, Weddings, Graduations, Diplomas, hearing certain poems.

Raising children and all the enjoyment they bring, school days, picnics,

Trips, hugs, laughter, tears, church, teaching them about God and praying over them.

Watching your children grow up and leave home.

Saying goodbye.

The list is endless.

We can stop and go back, I love THE fond memories of my yesterdays. However, I love today and very excited about tomorrow. Why? God is in it! Thank the Lord, it is His love that sustains us and arranges our tomorrows. His love will send our way that which is best for us. Gloria Gaither said something that I remember, "In spite of everything, when I look back at where I have been, I see that what I am becoming is a whole lot further down the road from where I was." Your Yesterdays is the path that leads you into your tomorrows. Remember, what you are doing right now will be a memory for tomorrow. Make it a good one!

Joanie Buchanan

38

FEAR NOT

Scripture: Jeremiah 1: 17

"Thou therefore gird up thy loins, and arise, and speak unto them all that I command thee: be not dismayed at their faces, lest I confound thee before them."

Reflection: God gave a message to Jeremiah and told Him to obey and not to be intimidated or fearful by what his enemies would try to do. God spoke directly to Jeremiah and gave him a command to press forward with faith and not be afraid by what he saw.

Fear will paralyze your faith and cause you to doubt God and His Word. Like the Word says, "Fear has torment."

This is something that I have to deal with at times myself. If it were not for God's Holy Spirit, honestly, I do not know where I would be today. Whether anyone really knew it or not, when I was a young woman I was fearful, easily intimidated, and a list that is too long to mention.

As we continue to read these verses we get a sense that there is a battle taking place. God is giving Jeremiah these encouraging words to let him know that he will not be alone. God speaks to the prophet in verse 18 saying that He has made him a fortified city, an iron pillar, and a bronze wall against the whole land. God was going to give him supernatural strength which no threatening power would ever be able to conqueror.

Believe me, there will always be opposing forces in whatever God tells us to do. However, we have the power of the Holy Spirit to overcome. We have an enemy that does everything he can to stop us from doing God's will. I know what it is like to forge ahead in faith and then have people deliberately seek to intimidate you with words or actions, after God has already spoken in your heart.

Remember, God said, "Do not be dismayed." Whatever their motives, nonetheless, it is a spirit that tries to frighten us so we will give up. There is an adversary that hates God and will do what he can to redirect our focus. Satan works diligently to use anyone or anything, sometimes it can be the most unexpected ones. Stay alert to the enemy's devices!

God would say to His people this day, "Get up, keep the full armor of God on, and go forward in My plans, not yours or mans, then you will have My divine favor"

In closing let us not forget verse Jeremiah 1:19, They will fight against you, but they will not prevail against you; for I am with you", says Yahweh, "to rescue you."

Now that is a promise from God the Great I AM, receive it today. Whatever God asked of us we must just do it!

He will shelter us with protection and every enemy will have to answer to God when touching God's anointed. If we do not obey God, sooner or later there will be some serious consequences.

39

HEAVENLY VISION

Scripture: Acts 26:16-19

> But rise, and stand upon thy feet: for I have
> appeared unto thee for this purpose, to make thee
> a minister and a witness both of these things
> which thou hast seen, and of those things in the
> which I will appear unto thee;   Delivering thee
> from the people, and from the Gentiles, unto
> whom now I send thee, To open their eyes, and to
> turn them from darkness to light, and from the
> power of Satan unto God, that they may receive
> forgiveness of sins, and inheritance among them
> which are sanctified by faith that is in me.
> Whereupon, O king Agrippa, I was not
> disobedient unto the heavenly vision:"

Reflection: It is one thing to receive a heavenly vision;
it is another to obey what is seen or heard in a vision.
One of the greatest lessons to be learned from the life

of Paul was his obedience to the written and spoken Word.

The apostle Paul goes on to point out that the heavenly vision is, "that they should repent and turn to God, and do works meet for repentance." (Mt 26:20). We must preach the full counsel of God. And today we must be equally diligent in proclaiming the Good News of the Gospel. I know for me, there have been times when I wanted to turn go home and lay down the heavenly calling given to me. Yet, Paul is such an example as to how we are to move forward with the Heavenly   Vision.

There will be temporary set-backs but there is no stopping for God's called out ones. Some of the greatest miracles of my life have been right when I was at the lowest point of my ministry.

Our problem is that some of us have not heeded the instructions that have been given to us from the Word of God. Hence, our vision is limited. We are content and not hungry for the things of God.

Amos the Prophet said in Amos 8:11,

"Behold, the days come, saith the Lord GOD, that I will send a famine in the land, not a famine of bread, nor a thirst for water, but of hearing the words of the LORD:"

Oh, that we might search the Scriptures, seeking the wisdom and blessing of God upon our lives by listening to the Word and doing what God says.

When He speaks to us, what a tremendous responsibility it places upon us to obey! God will not lead us from one step to another in our Christian walk until we have learned to obey the first step. His will for our lives is revealed only when we are willing to obey.

40

HOW DID I GET HERE?

Scripture Psalm 18:6

> In my distress I called upon the Lord, and cried
> unto my God: he heard my voice out of his
> temple, and my cry came before him, even into his
> ears.

Reflection: Have you ever found yourself in a place
you never envisioned you would be? Have you said,
"O God, how did I get here?"

The enemy of your soul can be so deceptive you can
get in trouble before you realize it. You know if you
allow him to, he will chip away at your life until you
become weak and faint-hearted. Nevertheless, you
continue like stubborn sheep trying to find the green
pastures you thought were just ahead. From a distance
the other pastures look so inviting that you continue
on a pathway following what you perceive instead of
what is known. Yet God, our Great Shepherd, has

warned time and again, "Stay away from those forbidden pastures." The land looks fruitful but it is barren and the enemies has set up ambushes. This path is the way of disobedience and only leads to an eventual future filled with destruction for you.

You began to rationalize in your own mind, "It has taken me awhile to get here and I am too tired to turn back, my body is tired and weary from the journey. My body racked with hunger, I cannot go another mile. What will people say? Surely, I cannot tell anyone about this messed up life, would they really care to know anyway? It seems no one was there for me when I really needed them and who's there for me now? How do I get back to where I was?"

Deep in your heart you know this is the wrong choice from the path God had laid out for you, "Now what is one to do with this messed up, broken life?" Is it for me to continue on, hoping that just ahead the right place that I have so desperately been looking for all the time will be there? You try to convince yourself that turning around is too hard. It is too late to try to start again, the heart becomes so heavy that you began to sob fearfully, "God, help me in this awful dilemma." God's Word, that has been dormant in your heart and mind for such a long time, starts to explode in your Spirit. David experienced this. As you read his cry it is so intense you can almost hear him, "I cried unto the Lord and he heard my cry and he delivered me." Once more the presence and the power of the Great Shepherd washes over your soul. There is a flood of living water that brings life to the barren areas. Let God's Word feed your barren and dry soul.

How sweet to be back into the arms of the Great Shepherd. Your vision is no longer blurred and now your eyes are open so that the green pastures were not what you thought that were. Life comes from a deeper spring with a greater capacity to see things as God sees them, no person on this earth can ever fulfill or satisfy that inner most being of your soul. It is the Good Shepherd that we must rely on for all things. What we think for a moment is enticing to our flesh is nothing but a false delusion in the recesses of our own carnal thinking.

God is here, if you are like that person, stop, turn around and go back where you left God. He is waiting!

41

LOVING GOD'S WAY

Scripture: 1 Corinthians 13:4-8 (WEB)

> Love is patient and is kind; love doesn't envy.
> Love doesn't brag, is not proud, 5 doesn't behave
> itself inappropriately, doesn't seek its own way, is
> not provoked, takes no account of evil; 6 doesn't
> rejoice in unrighteousness, but rejoices with the
> truth; 7 bears all things, believes all things, hopes
> all things, endures all things. 8 Love never fails.
> But where there are prophecies, they will be done
> away with. Where there are various languages, they
> will cease. Where there is knowledge, it will be
> done away with.

Reflection: I discovered a long time ago that it is not
within my own personal control to love as God as
commanded me to love. Self-help seminars and books

were very short lived. I tried to get outside assistance in changing who I was, but to no avail on my part. Self-help seminars never worked for me. It all sounded good, but later I ended up more discouraged than before.

What do I do? How can I love when I do not choose to love others? When someone hurts me, speaks lies against me, judges me inaccurately or throws stones at me when I fall short, how can I love that person?

In seeking God, He always assures me that it is through the power of His Holy Spirit that I can love, conquer and overcome when I surrender my will to Him. The Greek word for God's love is Agape, it is that unconditional love that lets us see through God's eyes in every circumstance we face in life.

Once the will submits and obeys what He has told us to do, it releases us to discover and develop what God has imparted in our hearts. Within the security of God's awesome power, we discover in our innermost being a wealth of wisdom. It is a deep profound capability far beyond what the human nature can create. In the security of His love we are set free. It is not because there is an eternal law that makes me free, but because the love of God has been shed abroad in my heart. God's love frees and is liberating to all who will surrender to Him. People are seeking freedom. It is God, and God alone, that sets our hearts free to do what we were put on this earth to do and achieve.

The absolute fact of finding God's love was unbelievable. I must tell you it changed my World; His lifetime of promises leads me on to a life course that is continually changing my heart.

God has given me confidence, strength and

freedom to do what I could have never done, had I not surrendered to Christ. I truly love because He first loved me.

Prayer: "Father, we submit our will to you and ask that you wake us up to the things that are given to us by your Holy Spirit. Let us first learn how to love you so we can love ourselves and our neighbor. We agree with your word that says in 1 Corinthians 16:14 (WEB),

Let all that you do be done in love.

And to love him with all the heart and with all the understanding and with all the strength, and to love one's neighbor as oneself, cis much more than all whole burnt offerings and sacrifices. Mark 12:33

Joanie Buchanan

42

TOO MUCH TO GAIN

Scripture: Hebrews 11:24-26 (WEB)

> By faith, Moses, when he had grown up, refused to be called the son of Pharaoh's daughter, 25 choosing rather to share ill treatment with God's people, than to enjoy the pleasures of sin for a time; 26 accounting the reproach of Christ greater riches than the treasures of Egypt; for he looked to the reward.

Reflection: Recompense means to give something by way of compensation (as for a service rendered or damage incurred to pay for all that one had to go through - Merriam-Webster's online dictionary).

What an awesome God, we owe him everything! He paid it all for us and yet when we make a choice to live for Him, he still keeps on giving to us.

Look at Moses. Moses found out that whatever he walked away from could never measure up to what

God would do for him. He was raised with a silver spoon in his mouth. He could have inherited all the riches of Egypt. It is hard to comprehend the luxuriousness of his surroundings and all he had at his disposal. I have heard that Pharaoh's Kingdom was worth over twenty billion dollars. That is a huge inheritance. Most of us might say, "What a fantastic future!" If we are thinking of only temporal possessions. What words of wisdom would you have given Moses? "Keep the inheritance, Moses, there is not a thing you can do to help those Israelites." Or, would you say, "Moses, following God is much more rewarding, now and for all eternity."?

Moses was recognized throughout the known world of his time as the grandson of Pharaoh. Yet, as he looked at the ill treatment of his people from the borders of the palace, it was a scene that gripped his heart. I am sure after much observation and meditation, Moses made his choice to be identified with his people. He saw that all the pomp and glory of his environment was nothing compared to serving God. Moses saw it as gain and not a loss. He considered the consequences of his future and saw that living for God would give back more than he could ever possess in Pharaoh's court.

Now, let's ask ourselves a few questions: How much would we be willing to let go of if it was standing in the way of our commitment to God? Is our identity and self-worth wrapped up in an inheritance, checkbook, bank account, person, or lifestyle? As God's child, if we are not careful, the temporal things of this world can become stumbling blocks in our total dedication to God. If those things are our only security, then we have missed what Moses discovered. Where will it get us in the long run, to spend all of our time and efforts on having stuff, if we leave God out of our lives?

Moses had to make a choice, he must walk away from the wealth of Egypt if he was going to identify himself with the poor and downtrodden Israelites, who just happened to be God's chosen people.

Security, identity and self-worth are characterized in Christ. We might quickly say, "I will agree with that," however, test your actions by God's Word and see if you have the faith of Moses. He saw that he had too much to gain by identifying with God's people.

Do you know Jesus as your personal Savior? If your answer is no, is it worth selling your soul for the fleeting enjoyments of this sinful world? Understand that the Messiah offers greater wealth than all the treasures of this world. What is your soul worth?

> But seek ye first the kingdom of God, and his righteousness; and all these things shall be added unto you. Matthew 6:33

> And every one that hath forsaken houses, or brethren, or sisters, or father, or mother, or wife, or children, or lands, for my name's sake, shall receive an hundredfold, and shall inherit everlasting life. Matthew 19:29

Joanie Buchanan

43

A SOLITARY PLACE

Scriptures: Mark 1:35 (WEB)

> Early in the morning, while it was still dark, he
> rose up and went out, and departed into a deserted
> place, and prayed there.

Reflection: It is imperative that Christians retreat from
the noise of their busy lifestyle and get alone with the
purpose of seeking God. If Jesus retreated, surely, we
must follow His example. If Christians would stop
daily to commune alone with God, we would share
fresh insight right from the heart of God. To be still is
imperative!

I believe the time apostle Paul spent in prison alone
with God gave him deeper spiritual insight. If he would
have had more free time to go about as he pleased, we
might not have had the letters of Paul today. That
journey of solitude gave him an open door to reach the
world. God knows what He is doing even when we do

not seem to have a clue.

We could also call on Moses, Elijah and David to give us testimonies of their times of solitude with God. Moses was on the back side of the desert when God spoke to him through the burning bush; David was out in the field watching sheep and writing Psalms; Elijah discovered God tends to whisper, as he was at the entrance of a cave. Those who walk with God will tell you, God does not ordinarily shout to make Himself known.

In our seclusion from the many sounds of the world, we can definitely hear the sounds of heaven. Yes, God can speak anywhere, but it is imperative that we get away and retreat from the busy lives most of us have chosen to live. Just find a quiet place and be still! If you do not linger long enough, you might hear Him say, "Don't go yet!" God loves for us to spend time with Him.

The two years my family and I spent in Alaska has proven to be much more profitable than I ever thought it would be.

My memories are still so vivid about my personal experiences while there. I have had to ask God to forgive me for the times I complained about being so far away from the rest of my family. I found myself at times crying and saying, "God, I feel like I am in a foreign land and totally isolated from my children and grandchildren."

Today, I still share my experiences learned while in Alaska. The stories are fruitful to those who hear what God taught me about solitude. My point is, "do not despise the times of isolation." God will do whatever He must to get the attention of His children. God wants us to reflect His image.

The one you spend the most time with is the one that you will imitate. If we commit to times of silence and solitude with God, our discipline will soon become our desire and our desire will turn into our delight. Jesus, our example:

> When Jesus heard it, He departed from there by boat to a deserted place by Himself. But when the multitudes heard it, they followed Him on foot from the cities. Matthew 14:13

> Then Jesus came with them to a place called Gethsemane, and said to his disciples, "Sit here, while I go there and pray." Matthew 26:36

Jesus went to a deserted place. Luke 4:42

Jesus went to the wilderness. Luke 5:16

Jesus instructs us to go "enter" our closets and shut the door to pray in secret, in solitude. Matthew 6:6

44

UNVEILING GOD'S GLORY: THE TRANSFIGURATION OF JESUS

Scripture: Luke 9:28-31

> And it came to pass about an eight days after these
> sayings, he took Peter and John and James, and
> went up into a mountain to pray. And as he
> prayed, the fashion of his countenance was
> altered, and his raiment was white and glistering.
> And, behold, there talked with him two men,
> which were Moses and Elias: Who appeared in
> glory, and spake of his decease which he should
> accomplish at Jerusalem.

Reflection: Mountain top experiences are also a part of
God's plan to unveil His glory.

"Glory" in Hebrew is Kabod which means heavy
or weighty. Have you experienced the presence of the
Lord when it has been hard to stand? I have
experienced His strong and powerful presence, and it

is always wonderful!

"Glory" in Greek is Doxa, which means, in simple terms, that which gives a proper opinion of someone or something. God's glory reveals to us who God is and gives us a proper opinion of who He is. The Word says that even "the heavens are telling of the Glory of God."

The Transfiguration gives us the appearance of His glory: Nearing the crucifixion of Jesus, He leaves Caesarea Philippi and travels about fourteen miles to Mt Hermon with Peter, James and John; Jesus often went to the mountain to pray however, this mountain trip was a little different. While Jesus was praying, the Glory cloud appeared which has always been a part of Israel's history. In the Old Testament it was the pillar of cloud by day and fire by night that led the Israelites.

This same cloud covered and filled the Tabernacle, it descended when the tablets of the law where given to Moses. This Glory cloud appeared when Solomon dedicated the Temple. Now, here is the same cloud appearing on Mt. Hermon sealing the approval of God's Son with what He commissioned Him to do. Jesus knew He was in the will of the Father and He must go on to His destination, the cross of Calvary.

Here on this mountain Jesus was transfigured and His appearance changed. Light came from His body and glowed outward. That, my friends, is a Mountain Top experience, when the Glory of the Lord is present. This occurrence represents the picture of the Son of Man wrapped in the Glory of God. What a great hope for now and the future that the fulfillment of all of His Glory is not just past and present but is also futuristic as stated in the Bible,

> For the Son of man shall come in the glory of his Father with his angels; and then he shall reward every man according to his works. Matthew 16:27

On this mountain top Moses and Elijah appeared and talked with Jesus, it was only fitting that they would be there to embark upon the New Covenant with Jesus. It was the dawning of a New Day. Moses and Elijah represented the Law and the Prophets, but now the Old Covenant was being fulfilled in Jesus' death.

Moses and Elijah were powerful subjects of God but they were never to be equal with Jesus. Peter should have been quiet but, being impetuous and a man of action, he made a mistake. He wanted to just linger there and make a monument. Have you felt that way when times with God have been so overwhelming, you just want to stay and not leave? At that moment, the Glory Cloud covered the disciples and God said,

> "This is My Beloved Son in whom I am well pleased." Luke 9:35

> Arise, shine; for thy light has come, and the glory of the LORD has risen upon you. Isaiah 60:1

Prayer: Lord, we want your Glory to be revealed in us. Just like the Glory Cloud covered each one in the Scripture cover us Lord through and through with your Glory. Talk to us and let us recognize only what You have called us to do. We yield to You and want to make a difference in the world You have called us to. Our faces are unveiled, we want to see Your Glory, now transform us daily into the same image from glory to glory, as Your Spirit reigns over us. Like Moses cried,

"Lord, show us your Glory."

Scriptures: Like Moses and Paul

> "I pray Thee, show me Thy glory! And enlighten the eyes of heart so that I may know what are the riches of the glory of Thy inheritance in the saints. Exodus 33:18, Ephesians 1:18

> But whenever one turns to the Lord, the veil is taken away. 17 Now the Lord is the Spirit and where the Spirit of the Lord is, there is liberty. 18 But we all, with unveiled face seeing the glory of the Lord as in a mirror, are transformed into the same image from glory to glory, even as from the Lord, the Spirit. 2 Corinthians 3:16-18 (WEB)

> Yahweh's glory shall be revealed, and all flesh shall see it together; for the mouth of Yahweh has spoken it." Isaiah 40:5 (WEB)

> "For the earth will be filled with the knowledge of the glory of the Lord as the waters cover the sea." Habakkuk 2:14

> The Word became flesh, and lived among us. We saw his glory, such glory as of the one and only Son of the Father, full of grace and truth. John 1:14

45

GOD MY HEALER

Scripture: James 5:15

> And the prayer of faith shall save the sick, and the
> Lord shall raise him up; and if he have committed
> sins, they shall be forgiven him.

Reflection: Praising Him for my deliverance!

In my late forties I was suddenly faced with pain I
had never experienced before. My family and I began
praying, but the pain continued to persist. After
several days of excruciating and unbearable pain, I
asked my husband to take me to a doctor. I felt I could
not endure it any longer. I was able to get an
appointment with a specialist and my husband
accompanied me to the appointment.

After I described to the doctor all that was going on
in my body, he did a preliminary examination and then
some extensive testing. He promised me they would
let me know the results in a few days.

A few days later I received a telephone call from the nurse who said, "Joanie we need you to come in." She tried to explain the test results in terms I could understand, but honestly it frightened me and confused me even more. The pain was not going away it has lasted for weeks. I found it very difficult to have faith.

The enemy did not waste any time in seeking to minimize my faith in God. Fear gripped me so tightly that I wondered how I was going to be able to deal with this unwanted news. The pain, of course, intensified my fears. The pain meds prescribed for me did very little to make me feel comfortable.

I was scheduled to go back to the doctor for more testing. I remember asking my daughter if she would go with me since my husband could not make the appointment that day. I prayed more and more as the appointment drew near; and my faith was strengthened through prayer.

Also, incredibly, my pain (after weeks of hurting) was subsiding. When the doctor walked into the room I asked if he believed in miracles. He said he did. As he was cutting off more tissue for testing, I kept repeating, "You are not going to find anything. God has healed me." I have to admit there was another voice trying to overpower my words and thoughts; but I would not submit to it.

After that appointment, I was instructed to go downstairs and check into the hospital. I talked myself into going to the admissions office. As I was sitting there talking to the admittance clerk, all of a sudden, I just got up and told her I was not going to do this and walked out.

I knew I did not have the faith and strength on my

own to walk through this difficult time, but I knew God would help me through it. I told my husband I am not going into the hospital.

A few days later the nurse had not called me to ask why I had not followed through with the physician's orders to check into the hospital. I had not heard the results of the last procedure done in his office. With that in mind, I called the nurse and said, 'Have you gotten any results back on Joan Buchanan?' Her response was, "Joan, the doctor and I have just now reviewed your test results. We have been trying to put our heads together on this, "all the tests are normal!" Well, the rest is history. I praised God with her on the phone and continued to praise God for His faithfulness and healing power.

His grace is always sufficient for everything we face in this life. To God be the Glory, Great things He has done!! I love you Lord.

46

READY OR NOT

Scripture: Proverbs 22:3

A prudent man foreseeth the evil, and hideth himself: but the simple pass on, and are punished.

Reflection: Jesus reveals His truth to us and we need to be prepared for the future.

Truth # 1

Jesus talked a great deal about the future. I Hear people say, "I am not concerned about the end times I just live each day for Jesus and leave it up to Him."

Some say, "No one knows anyway." Nothing could be further from the Bible truth. We need to heed the warnings.

Jesus wants His followers to know what's coming. That is why He spent so much time talking about it. It is crystal clear from his teachings that Jesus wants His followers to know what is ahead. He said "But take heed behold, I have told you everything in advance." Do not let anyone convince you that Jesus did not bother with the future. "Heaven and Earth will Pass away, but my Words will never pass away."

Truth #2

The Jews Missed it. Jesus rebuked the self-righteous Pharisees for their blindness. Jesus was performing signs all around them. He said,

> "O ye hypocrites, ye can discern the face of the sky; but can ye not discern the signs of the times?" Matthew 16:1-3

The Nation of Israel as a whole was blinded because they did not recognize the signs. People back then where not a whole lot different than today. They would not think of missing the evening weather on the news. However, they neglect the signs of the coming future events as foretold in Scripture.

Truth #3

The Bible talks about the future. We to change the way we live in the present. There are at least 353 prophecies that have already been fulfilled concerning Jesus Christ, Jesus said,

> "Lo, I come: in the volume of the book it is written of me." Psalm 40:7

> "The testimony of Jesus is the spirit of prophecy."

Revelation 19:10

"All things must be fulfilled, which were written in the Law of Moses, and in the prophets, and in the psalms, concerning me." Luke 24:44

"For had ye believed Moses, ye would have believed me: for he wrote of me." John 5:46

We are just as far down as we can go. Economically, socially morally and spiritually. We are going to the bottom and walking in the drag of this thing –Hopeless despair with no place to go but up. People are crying out on the earth and things are beginning to move. Jews are at the Wailing Wall---Calling their Messiah to come. The devil is in retreat and on his way down.

As we journey through life, how do we know that we are getting close to the end? We rely on signs along the way, each one announcing that we have come closer to the destination. Likewise, as we go through history, we see events along the way that mark our progress and assure us that the end is drawing near.

There were signs of the times before the first coming of Christ and we have signs of His second coming.

DO NOT MISS YOUR PRESENCE AND LOSE YOUR FUTURE

47

SPIRITUAL SUCCESS

Scripture: Joshua 6:1-9

Now Jericho was straitly shut up because of the children of Israel: none went out, and none came in. 2 And the Lord said unto Joshua, See, I have given into thine hand Jericho, and the king thereof, and the mighty men of valour. 3 And ye shall compass the city, all ye men of war, and go round about the city once. Thus shalt thou do six days. 4 And seven priests shall bear before the ark seven trumpets of rams' horns: and the seventh day ye shall compass the city seven times, and the priests shall blow with the trumpets. 5 And it shall come to pass, that when they make a long blast with the ram's horn, and when ye hear the sound of the trumpet, all the people shall shout with a great shout; and the wall of the city shall fall down flat, and the people shall ascend up every man straight before him.

6 And Joshua the son of Nun called the priests, and said unto them, Take up the ark of the covenant, and let seven priests bear seven trumpets of rams' horns before the ark of the Lord. 7 And he said unto the people, Pass on, and compass the city, and let him that is armed pass on before the ark of the Lord. 8 And it came to pass, when Joshua had spoken unto the people, that the seven priests bearing the seven trumpets of rams' horns passed on before the Lord, and blew with the trumpets: and the ark of the covenant of the Lord followed them. 9 And the armed men went before the priests that blew with the trumpets, and the rereward came after the ark, the priests going on, and blowing with the trumpets.

Reflection: To be all God called you to be obey His Word.

There is a common desire within every person to feel successful. We often measure our worth on the basis of how successful we are. How we measure that success is often based on a worldly standard rather than a godly standard. Success by the world's standard often means luxury, wealth, possessions, achievements, notoriety, fame, and beauty. If we measure our lives by the world's standards we will have an inaccurate and incomplete view of whether or not we're successful.

God's formula for success is completely unlike the world's formula. And His formula works for every person, in every situation, whether it's at school, in our business, our families, or our church. The pathway to success cannot be traveled by anyone who does not practice God's formula for success. These principles are taken from Joshua 1:6-9.

Devote yourself to using your time and energy in the best way possible: pursuing God's purposes for your life. Respond to God's love for you by expressing your love for Him, committing to faithfully being as productive as possible every day of your life. Live in one-day segments of faithful obedience, doing the best you can each new day to do whatever you sense God calling you to do with your life. Then renew your commitment to serve God when you wake up to another fresh day.

As the world sees success, it is the achievement of a social status, completing a goal, reaching an objective or the achievement of an action in a specified set of time. Success to those in the world means achieving something that is useful in this life on earth. Success as God sees it is something that is achieved that is of infinite, eternal value in this life and in the life to come. That is a huge difference indeed. The Bible describes success in a much different way than the world does.

> Blessed is the man that walketh not in the counsel of the ungodly, nor standeth in the way of sinners, nor sitteth in the seat of the scornful. 2 But his delight is in the law of the Lord; and in his law doth he meditate day and night. 3 And he shall be like a tree planted by the rivers of water, that bringeth forth his fruit in his season; his leaf also shall not wither; and whatsoever he doeth shall prosper. Psalm 1:1-3

> This Book of the Law shall not depart from your mouth, but you shall meditate on it day and night, so that you may be careful to do according to all

that is written in it. For then you will make your way prosperous, and then you will have good success. Joshua 1:8 (WEB)

If you will study these verses you will find these principles. A great formula for spiritually success

Principle #1: Preparation Exodus 33:11 Prayer. As a young aide to Moses, Joshua met with God in the tent of meeting.

Principle #2: The Command

Principle #3: Obey Instructions

Principle #4: Previsions are promised

Principle #5: Strong and Courageous

Principle #6: Stay Focused

Principle #7: Success comes from God at all times

Principle # 8: Speak the Word

Principle # 9: Meditate

Principle #10: No Fear. God is with you.

Prayer of Success: Nehemiah 1:11 (WEB)

Lord, I beg you, let your ear be attentive now to the prayer of your servant, and to the prayer of your servants, who delight to fear your name; and please prosper your servant today, and grant him mercy in the sight of this man." Now I was cup bearer to the king.

Joanie Buchanan

48

A TINY GIFT
STRANGELY WRAPPED
SILENTLY DELIVERED

Scripture: Luke 2:7

> And she brought forth her firstborn son, and
> wrapped him in swaddling clothes, and laid him in
> a manger; because there was no room for them in
> the inn.

Reflection: This article caught my eye. In the birth of
Jesus, God has delivered an indescribable gift to us.
The baby Jesus comes wrapped in prophecy

Some people seem to have a lot of fun wrapping.
They put one box after another inside one box after
another, each one carefully wrapped with ribbon to
bring you from one massive gift down to a tiny ring.
And who hasn't had that experience. And some gifts
you cannot seem to hide even though you wrapped
them carefully.

How do you wrap an indescribable gift? What material do you use? Mary wrapped him in cloth. She came prepared for that. First you wrap him in prophecy. God doesn't just suddenly drop Jesus Christ out of heaven to earth. I mean he prepares man for his coming hundreds of years ahead of time. Listen to a few.

"Therefore Jehovah himself will give you a sign. Behold, a virgin will be with child and bear a son, and she will call his name Immanuel. Isaiah 7:14

You wrap something indescribable in something as powerful as prophecy and you have people anticipating his arrival.

6 For unto us a child is born, unto us a son is given: and the government shall be upon his shoulder: and his name shall be called Wonderful, Counsellor, The mighty God, The everlasting Father, The Prince of Peace. 7 Of the increase of his government and peace there shall be no end, upon the throne of David, and upon his kingdom, to order it, and to establish it with judgment and with justice from henceforth even for ever. Isaiah 9:6-7

Turn to Isaiah 53. Isaiah is at a loss. He's asking who will believe this message. He's living among a people of unclean lips. He knows his times. He says: "Who has believed our message? And to whom has the arm of the Lord been revealed?" Who's waiting on tiptoes for the coming of the Messiah? Describe him for us, Isaiah. He will grow up before him like a tender shoot, like a root out of parched ground; He has no stately form or majesty that we should look upon him. that we should be attracted to him. That isn't what made Jesus Christ significant. He looked like any other Jew of his day. As a boy he looked like any other carpenter's son. His appearance had nothing majestic about it. There was no shining glow about him. It was God who came in the form of a man, don't forget, not man in the form of God.

He drove a nail just like anyone else. He worked with wood like anyone else. He. Why, he was despised and forsaken, a man of sorrows and acquainted with grief. We did not esteem him. How do you wrap an indescribable gift? He was wrapped in prophecy.

Thank God for His marvelous Gift. We have nothing we can give in return. All He asked was, "Come unto me, all ye that labor and are heavy laden, and I will take your burdens and your sins, and set you free."

What an exchange! Nobody could do that but Father God. And we are His witnesses in this dark hour that Christ took our burden of sin and gave us joy and peace instead.

This willingness to do His will at all costs is one of the most important attitudes we can have. Then, God can freely manifest His Life and His Love through us.

> Search me, O God, and know my heart: try me, and know my thoughts: And see if there be any wicked way in me, and lead me in the way everlasting. Psalm 139:23-24

49

THE WISE WOMAN

Scripture: Proverbs 31:11-31 (WEB)

The heart of her husband trusts in her.
　　He shall have no lack of gain.
12 She does him good, and not harm,
　　all the days of her life.
13 She seeks wool and flax,
　　and works eagerly with her hands.
14 She is like the merchant ships.
　　She brings her bread from afar.
15 She rises also while it is yet night,
　　gives food to her household,
　　and portions for her servant girls.
16 She considers a field, and buys it.
　　With the fruit of her hands, she plants a
vineyard.
17 She arms her waist with strength,
　　and makes her arms strong.

18 She perceives that her merchandise is profitable.

Her lamp doesn't go out by night.

19 She lays her hands to the distaff,
and her hands hold the spindle.

20 She opens her arms to the poor;
yes, she extends her hands to the needy.

21 She is not afraid of the snow for her household;
for all her household are clothed with scarlet.

22 She makes for herself carpets of tapestry.
Her clothing is fine linen and purple.

23 Her husband is respected in the gates,
when he sits among the elders of the land.

24 She makes linen garments and sells them,
and delivers sashes to the merchant.

25 Strength and dignity are her clothing.
She laughs at the time to come.

26 She opens her mouth with wisdom.
Faithful instruction is on her tongue.

27 She looks well to the ways of her household,
and doesn't eat the bread of idleness.

28 Her children rise up and call her blessed.
Her husband also praises her:

29 "Many women do noble things,
but you excel them all."

30 Charm is deceitful, and beauty is vain;
but a woman who fears Yahweh, she shall be praised.

31 Give her of the fruit of her hands!
Let her works praise her in the gates!

Reflection: The longer we walk with the Lord the more seasoned we should become. And the easier we should become. Let's not make this a legalistic list. Just know that these are words from God's Word and that the Spirit of God will make it a part of our lives as we allow him to trim out the rough edges.

In Proverbs 31:1-19 "Spoil" has to do with the goods taken in warfare, or by violence, and the ideal woman is such a manager that her husband can trust her to make do with what he brings in and will not constantly nag him until he resorts to violent means to satisfy her greed for worldly possessions. He trusts her wise management of the household so that he needs not to try to do his work and hers both.

Proverbs 31:20-23 Means that due to the diligence of his wife, the husband will rise to a place of influence and power. This is a perk of the virtuous. This speaks of the dignity of this woman: she is the wife of a city judge, for the gates were where courts of justice were held, and cases of dispute were heard and settled. He is known, not only by the clothes he wears, but for his wisdom in judgment, of which his wife is a partaker, and for his exercise of authority over his household, in which she shares. They both reflect well on the other. Every married couple will reflect on each other for good or for ill, according to their character. Here, the suggestion appears to be that his wife reflects well on him in his official position.

In Proverbs 31:24-31 is a list some of her attributes.

1. She Must Have a Hatred for Evil

Wisdom will have an increase sensitivity toward evil. To Wisdom evil just cannot be accepted. I believe the Provers 31 women will not lower her Godly standards and for that she recognizes deception when she sees it. She sees evil when it is masked as rebellion against God and His true path. God says he will show us the way to go and we can discern that which is good and that which is evil.

2. Restrained Lips and a Controlled Tongue

"She openeth her mouth with wisdom; and in her tongue is the law of kindness." Proverbs 12:26

"The mouth of the just bringeth forth wisdom: but the froward tongue shall be cut out. Proverbs 10:31

Discernment replaces chatter. There is a depth in her dialogue. Her timing is right, she says right thing at the right time. She will Pause. Think. Ponder before she answers. Silence can sometimes be our friend. "The tongue is truly the index of the heart."

3. Emotional Stability

"Strength and honor or her clothing." Proverbs 21:25

There is a leveling out of emotions. The greater the revelation the greater the constancy. The women who lives cheap does not ponder the path of life. She has way too many highs and lows. A woman with low self-esteem has a feeling of uncertainty. She has a of lack of self-confidence.

"She does not ponder the path of life; her ways wander, and she does not know it." Proverbs 5:6

There is a leveling out of emotions. The greater the revelation the greater the constancy. The woman who lives cheap does not ponder the path of life. She has way too many highs and lows. A woman with low self-esteem has a feeling of uncertainty. She has a lot of lack of self-confidence.

Wisdom rests in the heart of a man of understanding, but it makes itself known even in the midst of fools.

4. A Wise Woman has a Listening Ear – A Teachable Spirit

This wise woman is always ready to pay attention. She is eager to absorb and has a heart of meekness. Does not have to take charge. It is really beautiful to connect with someone who loves truth because their face just lights up.

The ear that listens to reproof lives, and will be at home among the wise. [32] He who refuses correction despises his own soul, but he who listens to reproof gets understanding. [33] The fear of Yahweh teaches wisdom. Before honor is humility. Proverbs 15:31-33 (WEB)

5. Her Heart is Free of Jealousy

One must learn to be comfortable being who they are. Free of envy. And jealousy.

Do we not know that the same Holy Spirit that anoints one can also do it for another? How we limit the Spirit of God.

> Let not your heart envy sinners, but continue in the fear of the Lord all the day. Surely there is a future, and your hope will not be cut off. Proverbs 23:17-19

> Hear, my son, and be wise, and direct your heart in the way. Proverbs 24:1-4

> "Be not envious of evil men, nor desire to be with them, for their hearts devise violence, and their lips talk of trouble. By wisdom a house is built, and by understanding it is established; by knowledge the rooms are filled with all precious and pleasant riches."

Proverbs is one of my favorite Chapters in the Bible. It is not legalistic. We think we have to follow her in everything she does. The list I have given is some of the important attributes I have seen in this Proverbs 31 woman.

50

"57 CENTS"
LITTLE IS MUCH WHEN GOD IS IN IT!

Scripture: John 3:16 and John 15:13

GOD GAVE: "…His only begotten Son…"

JESUS GAVE: His life. Jesus said: "Greater love hath no man than this, that a man lay down his life for his friends." (John 15:13).

Reflection: Little is much when God is in it.

A sobbing little girl stood near a small church from which she had been turned away because it was "too crowded."

"I can't go to Sunday School." she sobbed to the pastor as he walked by. Seeing her shabby, unkept appearance, the pastor guessed the reason and, taking her by the hand, took her inside and found a place for her in the Sunday school class. The child was so happy that they found room for her that she went to bed that night thinking of the children who have no place to worship.

Some two years later, this child lay dead in one of the poor tenement buildings. Her parents called for the kind-hearted pastor who had befriended their daughter to handle the final arrangements. As her poor little body was being moved, a worn and crumpled red purse was found which seemed to have been rummaged from some trash dump. Inside was found 57 cents and a note, scribbled in childish handwriting, which read: "This is to help build the little church bigger so more children can go to Sunday School." For two years she had saved for this offering of love.

When the pastor tearfully read that note, he knew instantly what he would do. Carrying this note and the cracked, red pocketbook to the pulpit he told the story of her unselfish love and devotion. He challenged his deacons to get busy and raise enough money for the larger building.

But the story does not end there...

A newspaper learned of the story and published it. It was read by a wealthy realtor who offered them a parcel of land worth many thousands. When told that the church could not pay so much, he offered to sell it to the little church for 57 cents.

Church members made large donations. Checks came from far and wide. Within five years the little girl's gift had increased to 250,000.00---a huge sum for that time (near the turn of the century). Her unselfish love had paid large dividends.

When you are in the city of Philadelphia, look up Temple Baptist Church, with a seating capacity of 3,300. And be sure to visit Temple University, where thousands of students are educated. Have a look, too, at the Good Samaritan Hospital and at a Sunday School building which houses hundreds of beautiful children, built so that no child in the area will ever need to be left outside during Sunday school time.

In one of the rooms of this building may be seen the picture of the sweet face of the little girl whose 57 cents, so sacrificially saved, made such a remarkable history. Alongside of it is a portrait of her kind pastor, Dr. Russell H. Conwell, author of the book, *Acres of Diamonds*.

This is a true story, oddly enough I found this article on the wall in a children's classroom. I was speaking at a church and went in to study. This story goes to show WHAT GOD CAN DO WITH 57 CENTS!

51

CATCH THE LITTLE FOXES

Scripture: Song of Solomon 2:15

> Take us the foxes, the little foxes, that spoil the vines: for our vines have tender grapes.

Reflection: We have to make a determination – we're going to lay hold of the little foxes. God's got a harvest for us, He sows tares. When the vines are alive with new grapes, he sends out foxes. Today, we have to decide we're going to catch the foxes, before they destroy tomorrow's harvest.

Sometimes they are little squabbles within the body; little problems that arise between members. sometimes, it's the imaginary issues. "So-and-so just doesn't like me." Maybe she just had a bad day. A lot of times, the problems we perceive are just imaginary; things we come up with on our own. You may think is mad at you, and she might be clueless as to what's going on.

191

We have to put up our defenses against the foxes, now. Prepare ourselves. I've begun to see the tender grapes, appearing on the vine again. And as sure as the tender shoots spring forth… as sure as the blossoms appear… as sure as developing grapes burst out into a cluster, foxes appear.

We're serving a loving God, who sends the growth. But we're fighting a treacherous devil, who is determined to keep us from being fruitful. He's sending out the foxes. And make no mistake, the foxes will come. But look what the passage says about the foxes. Verse 15 calls them "little foxes."

The passage says, "Take us the foxes, the little foxes…" Most of the things that ruin vineyards, are little things. God help us; the little foxes.

It's like the vine is out of control, it's growing in a way that the enemy can't do one thing about. Jesus said, "I will build my church and the gates of hell will not prevail against it." And the vine strengthens we commit ourselves to prayer. We recognize that God will show us when we're dealing with a little Fox, if we'll just faithfully pray. We get into the Word of God. The Word that teaches us that our adversary the devil is roaming around like a roaring lion, if it had said "CAN" devour, that would imply ability. There's no question the devil can devour. But "MAY" implies permission.

The devil is roaming around looking for someone he's got permission to devour, we pray, and we get into the Word. And we have to decide, we're not going to be influenced by the little foxes when they do come. The little foxes come just as surely as the growth comes. As soon as fledgling grapes burst forth on the vine, the foxes appear. They begin gnawing on the green shoots. It only takes a few foxes loose in the vineyard, and the harvest is destroyed. A year lost; efforts hindered. Precious young growth forever devoured and carried away.

We have to make a determination – we're going to lay hold of the little foxes now. We're going to seize them. We're going to recognize when there is a fox loose trying to destroy growth. We're going to look for the tactics of the devil. We determine, we're going to walk circumspectly not as fools, but wise, redeeming the time for the days are evil.

52

GOD'S NATURE

Scripture: Philippians 3:12-16 (WEB)

Not that I have already obtained, or am already made perfect; but I press on, if it is so that I may take hold of that for which also I was taken hold of by Christ Jesus. 13 Brothers, I don't regard myself as yet having taken hold, but one thing I do. Forgetting the things which are behind, and stretching forward to the things which are before, 14 I press on toward the goal for the prize of the high calling of God in Christ Jesus. 15 Let us therefore, as many as are perfect, think this way. If in anything you think otherwise, God will also reveal that to you. 16 Nevertheless, to the extent that we have already attained, let us walk by the same rule. Let us be of the same mind.

Reflection: Let us seek God not only for our self but our family, our churches, friends, leaders, Nation and many other things. I am blessed and thankful for all the family that God has given me! Yet, God has asked me to remind each of us that we must spend time in prayer for them as we face a very exciting and challenging year.

My thoughts are on the coming days that we will be facing in this year. God has pressed on my heart once again to live out Galatians 5:16-23; It commands us to walk daily in the Spirit. Our life will become our Worship to God when daily we surrender to Him, everything will fit together like a puzzle when God is our focus

> But I say, walk by the Spirit, and you won't fulfill the lust of the flesh. 17 For the flesh lusts against the Spirit, and the Spirit against the flesh; and these are contrary to one another, that you may not do the things that you desire. 18 But if you are led by the Spirit, you are not under the law. 19 Now the deeds of the flesh are obvious, which are: adultery, sexual immorality, uncleanness, lustfulness, 20 idolatry, sorcery, hatred, strife, jealousies, outbursts of anger, rivalries, divisions, heresies, 21 envy, murders, drunkenness, orgies, and things like these; of which I forewarn you, even as I also forewarned you, that those who practice such things will not inherit God's Kingdom. 22 But the fruit of the Spirit is love, joy, peace, patience, kindness, goodness, faith, 23 gentleness, and self-control. Against such things there is no law. Galatians 5:16-23 (WEB)

Do any of these verses strike a chord within your heart? Wouldn't it be beyond wonderful to look ahead with a determined heart to truly be submitted to the Spirit of God on a continually basis. We like Paul would say,

> I have been crucified with Christ, and it is no longer I that live, but Christ living in me. That life which I now live in the flesh, I live by faith in the Son of God, who loved me, and gave himself up for me. Galatians 2:20 (WEB)

The Lord says,

> "Don't remember the former things, and don't consider the things of old. Behold, I will do a new thing. It springs out now. Don't you know it? I will even make a way in the wilderness, and rivers in the desert. Isaiah 43:18-19 (WEB)

As tomorrow dawns, it will be another day, a new opportunity, and once again another season to show our love and faith in Jesus to a world that so desperately needs the Savior.

As we journey forward, knowing that God already lives in the future and promises to provide us refreshment as we make the journey that is before us. I hear my Lord calling to make the most of our time as long as it last. How long is the journey ahead? Only God knows.

THE AUTHOR OF DEVOTIONALS
JOANIE BUCHANAN

Joanie started out with her husband in Bible School which put her on a course to teach God's Word. She and her husband have traveled extensively. They have pastored churches in Alaska, Colorado, Texas and Missouri. They have 4 children, 8 grandchildren and 3 great-grandchildren.

Joanie shares how God's Word gives timely instructions on how to walk out one's Christian faith day by day. She says that you can find all kinds of courses available on how to get motivated and spark initiative in starting a project. But let's extol the virtues of sticking with something day by day until it is finished. Or, hanging in when times get bumpy and the excitement fads away into discipline and guts. Many start the Christian life like a lightening flash, but how many in later life are finishing the course with sustained enthusiasm and vigor.

She shares the love and adoration that she has for Jesus Christ through teaching and speaking to diverse groups across the country. She has ministered in churches, Bible study groups, county jails, state prisons, juvenile centers, nursing homes, hospitals, parks; she also has worked in television, with her own program and for 8 years she has been in radio. Her heart is to see children, families and singles learn how to live out their faith through the teachings of God's Word which brings daily practical Christianity.

The desire of her heart is that God gets the glory in the journey He has ordained for her.

She says, "He is our Savior, healer, and soon coming King and she loves the path God has put her on.

My prayer is as you read these devotionals that God gave to me and it will encourage you. Your life's journey is ahead of you. Let's do some traveling together on this journey of Life for a few weeks. Every day we fight battles, there are times in our lives when we have been hit by blow after blow, and we feel crushed and shattered. During these occasions, it is easy to lose all hope. God does not want us to live out our daily existence depressed or hopeless. In His Word you can find comfort and assurance of his eternal blessings that will give us daily encouragement. Here is only one Bible verse for when you feel defeated.

Deuteronomy 20:4 "For the LORD your God is he that goeth with you, to fight for you against your enemies, to save you."

All for His Glory
Joanie Buchanan

Made in the USA
Lexington, KY
25 July 2018